PRAYING SAFE

The professional approach to protecting faith communities

GRANT CUNNINGHAM
JOSHUA GIDEON

Personal Security Institute, LLC

Praying Safe

The professional approach to protecting faith communities

By Grant Cunningham and Joshua Gideon

Published by Personal Security Institute LLC.

www.prayingsafe.com

COMING SOON: THE PRAYING SAFE WORKBOOK

There's a lot of detail work in the job of securing a worship community. Doing the right things, in the right order, and keeping track of it all can be a big job.

Our companion workbook will make that job easier! The **Praying Safe Workbook** combines blank forms, checklists, and step-by-step guides to doing all of the assessments and planning we talk about in **Praying Safe: The professional approach to protecting faith communities**.

The **Praying Safe Workbook** will be released in the first months of 2019, but you can get advance notice of the release by signing up to the mailing list!

Just go to this link:

www.getgrant.us/PSW

...and you'll be able to sign up for the mailing list and receive advance notification when the Workbook is available for purchase. In addition, we'll be sending complimentary pre-release copies to random members of the mailing list for their feedback. You may be the lucky one who gets a free copy!

(Don't worry, we'll treat your email address as confidential; it will not be sold to or shared with anyone else.)

CONTENTS

ACKNOWLEDGMENTS

From Joshua Gideon:

Thank you to my wife Aulana and daughter Allison for all your support and understanding during the writing of this book. I love you both and I treasure the time I get to spend with both of you.

A special thank you to my co-author Grant Cunningham. It is rare to find someone you can call a friend, even rarer to find a friend that you can call a mentor, and rarer still a friend you can write a book with and still call them a friend at the end of the project. Through all my mistakes, stubbornness, and confusion, he took this young writer under his wing and patiently led me on this journey. I am humbled and honored to call him my co-author. I am privileged to call him my friend.

From Grant Cunningham:

First, Joshua Gideon gets my undying appreciation (and admiration) for agreeing to write this book with me. His background in formal risk management, as well as his extensive executive protection experience, made him the ideal person to collaborate with. He was flexible when it was needed but stood firm where it was important. I couldn't have asked for a better writing partner — or friend.

As always, my wife Chris is a rock who takes care of things around the farm so that I can have uninterrupted research and writing time. Without her, I'd never get anything done!

A big thanks goes to our editor, Kathy Allard, who had a tough job to do integrating two very different writers into a cohesive whole. Her frank and incisive criticism was critical to producing a work Josh and I are both proud of.

Finally, we couldn't have made this happen without the members of our Launch Team, who graciously agreed to review the book prior to publication. They are: Joe Swartz, chris myers, John R. Dinkel, Angel C. Alvarez, Dr. David F. Simpson, Kevin H. Mowry, David W. Eldred, Ben Walton, Patrick S. Coons, Steve Antoine, Scott Reisenauer, John M. Hintermaier, George Prudden, John Flynn, James Nyffeler, Roddy Abshire, Michael A. Kelly, Dr. Greg Hutchens, Mark Chudzicki, and Dr. Terry Colley. Thank you all for your generous help in making this project a reality!

INTRODUCTIONS

Introduction by Grant Cunningham

In the first half of the 17th century, Catholics, Quakers, Episcopalians, Sephardic Jews, and others established the first religious congregations in what would become the United States. At the founding of our nation more than a century later, we institutionalized the right to worship freely (or to not worship at all) without government coercion. It was, in fact, one of the bedrock principles on which the founders based their Bill of Rights. Many of our early settlers came here specifically to avoid religious persecution in their home countries.

Today it would be difficult to find an American town of any size that did not have at least one religious organization within its boundaries. Worship, community, and charity are all part of the religious experience in the United States. People are often welcomed to worship and join the congregation without regard for their past or present sins; forgiveness is part of the bargain.

At the same time, people bring with them their own problems, anger, and hatred. Sometimes those ills boil over into the congregation. As a result, theft, assault, and murder have all happened in various denominations and sects across this country. Many of those, perhaps even most, could have been prevented or mitigated had the leadership of those congregations and communities made a commitment to do so.

Of course it's not just internal threats that congregations need to be concerned with. Houses of worship have been targets of intolerance and terrorism, not to mention the occasional random nut who decides they're an easy target — one that's unlikely to fight back. Sadly, they're often correct in their assumption.

Religious institutions, in fact, don't usually fight back, and many times don't even acknowledge their own weaknesses. Belief in the protection of a supreme being is part and parcel of faith, but it ignores the very real possibility that the gift they've been given is the means to take care of themselves.

As my co-author is fond of saying, anytime you encourage people to gather in confined spaces, you have a moral responsibility to ensure the safety and security of those people. While that responsibility may not be legal in nature (though the legal environment appears to be changing), religious communities deal in moral commitments. It seems disingenuous to preach moral responsibility from the pulpit but not put that into practice for the people seated in the room.

That's why Joshua and I decided to pool our expertise to write this book. For those congregations that have the moral conviction to acknowledge that their responsibility goes beyond what is written in their state's statute books, we hope to provide a framework around which they can build a safer environment for their congregants, their clergy, their staff, and ultimately their community.

. . .

Because it's the right thing to do.

Introduction by Joshua Gideon

It fascinates me how tradition and personal biases have shaped how religious groups deal with specific topics. As Grant and I began collaborating on the creation of this book, it became clear that we would need to address an elephant in the room.

That elephant is the resistance toward providing for the safety and security of the people these groups gather together to worship. There are many excuses for not dealing with this issue. Some of those we will discuss in detail later in this book. Regardless of religious tradition, we can't deny the moral responsibility that has been given to us to protect life.

We see this moral obligation to protect life as a principle of natural law. When the founders of the United States created documents declaring their independence, they felt it was important to emphasize the moral obligation to protect life: "We hold these Truths to be self-evident, that all Men are created equal, that they are endowed by their Creator with certain unalienable Rights, that among these are Life, Liberty, and the Pursuit of Happiness."

The framers pointed out that these rights are inherent. This means they are "involved in the constitution of or essential to the character of something." Consequently, inalienable rights are inherent in us because they refer to specific qualities that make us human beings. Without them, we lose our humanity. With no inherent right to life and liberty, we would be no different than animals.

. . .

We are unable to change our nature, so we are unable to rid ourselves of our essential qualities, such as the capacity to make moral choices. These qualities are the basis of our inalienable rights. The moral obligation to protect life is a principle that goes to the core of how God made us. It is at the core of what separates us from the beasts of this planet.

Far too many religious institutions do not want to address the excuses that prevent them from meeting this moral responsibility. They would rather accept the excuses than risk dealing with the consequences of pointing out the elephant sitting next to them. Fear of a drop in attendance and the resulting drop in revenue is likely the biggest motivating factor.

Leaders and members of religious organizations need to take a step back and assess if the reason they are not addressing this moral responsibility is based on immoral excuses. I can't think of any religions that promote money over moral obligation, and thus it's time we stop being hypocrites and take action to protect our own.

Who is this book written for?

We've designed this as a handbook for all those who are interested enough in their congregation's safety and security to get involved at some level. It's a guide to the process of risk management, how it's planned and implemented, and the jobs that need to be done to make that happen.

It's designed so that anyone, no matter whether they're interested in planning, organizing, or being a member of an actual security team, can pick it up and understand the entire process and where they fit in. It's more of a team manual than an individual guide, though everyone will likely find some tasks more suited to their interests than others.

. . .

There is a large amount of work to be done in any comprehensive safety and security program, and a wide range of skills are needed. In these pages we'll show the tasks that need to be done, who may be best suited for them, and how even the smallest contribution to the effort is important to the outcome.

About this book

This book is about using risk management principles to construct and implement a comprehensive security plan tailored to the needs of houses of worship. In it, we'll show how to identify potential targets, how to use intelligence to track possible threats, how to judge the amount of risk posed by those threats, and finally how to use all of that information to put protective measures in place.

This risk management approach to worship safety is what truly separates this book from others. Most sources of security information for faith communities take a "one size fits all" approach to protection. They do not account for the differences in our places of worship. A small Catholic parish in a rural community has very different needs than a large synagogue in a dense metropolitan area, which in turn requires a different approach than a Baptist church in a suburb.

We suggest that everyone involved read through the book completely before starting the exercises. It's important to understand the big picture, how the pieces fit together, and what each person involved will be doing. The process of risk management is actually fairly simple, but it can seem complex when trying to deal with the nuances of threats, targets, vulnerabilities, and mitigation.

Tolerance and respect

One of the authors is Jewish and the other is Protestant Christian, but both of us have respect for all religions and practices. We've therefore tried our best to use denominationally neutral language throughout, but must acknowledge it's sometimes very difficult to find a neutral term that applies to everyone equally.

Even knowing if we're offending another religion with any given word or phrase is almost impossible, and we apologize in advance for any unintended misapplication of words, phrases, terms, or references.

Except when it's specifically stated, it's fair to assume that everything in this text applies to church, synagogue, temple, mosque, and any other worship community or sanctuary equally.

We've also done our best to make the information itself applicable over a wide range of religious traditions. This is very difficult, because while we pride ourselves on being fairly aware of religions other than our own, we can't (and certainly don't) know the details of every religious tradition, practice, or custom.

We're fairly confident the material is usable for most mainstream religions in the United States, but there may be information that simply doesn't apply to some specific denominational practices. Should that happen, we welcome feedback in helping us to craft a future edition that speaks more accurately to a wider audience.

Gender assumptions

Almost everything in this book should be considered gender neutral. But in the interest of readability, we have adopted the masculine gender to describe people. This convenience should not be construed as implying that women are unsuitable for any part of the risk management process — nor should anyone make the dangerous assumption that attackers are always male!

About the authors

Grant Cunningham is an author, teacher, and consultant in the areas of self-defense, personal safety, home and family defense, and instructor development.

Grant has written a wide range of best-selling books and magazine articles on the subjects of firearms, defensive shooting, and preparedness, and has been featured or profiled in many magazines on those subjects.

He's been studying the fields of self-defense and personal preparedness since the early 1990s. In that pursuit, he's attended hundreds of hours of training in many different related fields, from defensive firearms to immediate trauma care to how predatory criminals think. He even did the coursework for a degree in Emergency Management to learn the state-of-the-art in planning for a wide range of potential hazards.

Grant served as director of security for his own congregation, where his job included regular meetings with police and FBI officials to learn about emerging and expanding threats. His experience in this area led him to consult on security and risk mitigation planning for other houses of worship.

He teaches workshops all over the United States in self-defense, home and family protection, and defensive shooting. He also writes a popular blog on these topics and is a frequent guest on radio shows and podcasts dealing with these topics.

. . .

Learn more about Grant at his site, www.grantcunningham.com.

Joshua Gideon is a security professional with expertise in physical security, executive protection, information technology security, risk management, compliance, and auditing. This wide range of experience in the security industry has allowed Josh the opportunity to work in several different fields, including banking, healthcare, and electrical utilities.

Prior to that, Josh spent years in the executive protection world as a Certified Dignitary Protection Agent, eventually working as an instructor teaching executive protection to others.

Josh uses his unique experience to teach and consult for businesses, churches, and critical infrastructure. He teaches his risk management-based classes and workshops all around the country and heads up the security team in his own congregation.

In 2013, Josh started "No Soft Targets" to help bring awareness to the vulnerable soft targets around us and demonstrate viable solutions to harden them. He is also an ordained minister and studying to be a Volunteer Chaplain.

More information about Josh and his current projects can be found at www.nosofttargets.com.

THE NEED FOR SECURITY IN HOUSES OF WORSHIP

The terrorist attacks in Mumbai, India over Thanksgiving weekend 2008 were a turning point for many people. They illustrated the ease with which those who wish to harm others can so easily attack soft targets with devastating effect.

A railway station, two hotels, a cafe, a religious facility, a cinema, a hospital, and a college were among the venues chosen by the well-prepared attackers. Most were what we call "soft targets" — those with very little security in place to prevent such an attack.

Since Mumbai, numerous attacks on places of worship have become a constant reminder that we must remain vigilant. Bad guys of various stripes will never stop focusing on soft targets, because they're easy pickings.

Places of worship are especially vulnerable, as many of them are not only soft targets, but they also check off many of the boxes in the "bad guy playbook":

- Many people together in a confined space — check.
- Open to the public and easily accessible — check.
- Religious or political affiliations that help make a bigger statement — check.
- Large amounts of cash and valuables present — check.

Sadly, those checks often add up to a very desirable target for criminals, terrorists, organized crime, hate groups, and active shooters. Later in this book, we'll discuss the specific targets — the things attackers are after — that increase the risk for places of worship.

Let's take a look at some fairly recent history and see if we can learn something about what we're facing.

A short history of notable attacks on places of faith

On June 30, 1974, a 23-year-old man named Marcus Chenault, armed with two pistols, entered Ebenezer Baptist Church in Atlanta. Witnesses indicated that he yelled, "I'm tired of all this" and opened fire.

Interviewed after his capture, Chenault claimed his original target was Martin Luther King Sr. But because she was closer, he decided to shoot Alberta King (Sr.'s wife and mother to Martin Luther King Jr.) instead. She died while sitting at the church organ. A church deacon was also killed in the attack, and one other person was wounded.

Mr. Chenault later explained that he shot King because "all Christians are my enemies." Evidently, prior to this event, Mr. Chenault — who was African-American — had decided that all black ministers were a menace to their people and that (his) God had told him to do it.

Many people today have forgotten this incident, or don't associate the event as an attack on a place of worship. It certainly wasn't the first time a church had been attacked. In 1963, four segregationists and Ku Klux Klan members bombed the 16th Street Baptist Church in Birmingham, Alabama. Three girls aged 14 and one aged 11 died that day. Twenty-two other people were injured.

It's not just Christian denominations, either. Another prominent attack occurred on August 9, 1991, when Jonathan Doody and Allessandro Garcia used a rifle and a shotgun to rob and kill nine people at the Wat Promkunaram Buddhist Temple in Waddell, Arizona. The victims' bodies were not found until a day later. At the time, it was considered the worst shooting in Arizona history.

On March 10, 1999, 22-year-old Shon Miller Sr. entered the New St. John Fellowship Baptist Church in Gonzales, Louisiana, and shot twice in the air as he yelled for everyone to get on the floor. Eyewitnesses recount that when his own two-year-old son called out for "Daddy", Miller shot his estranged wife — and then shot the boy.

Miller then walked down the aisle shooting others as they called out to God for help and tried to shield themselves in their pews. Witnesses said that he "calmly reloaded his pistol in the middle of the shooting and started shooting again." Police Chief Bill Landry called the scene "a nightmare" and that the panic in the faces of the congregation was "unbelievable."

More recently, the First Baptist Church in Sutherland Springs, Texas was attacked on a Sunday morning in 2017. Prior to entering the church, attacker Devin Kelley fired at the building from outside. He then entered the building and, similar to the shooting at St. John Fellowship, went down the aisle shooting people in the pews. Twenty-six people were killed and 20 more injured in the attack.

In 2006, the Seattle Jewish Federation was attacked by a Pakistani man armed with two pistols and a large knife. He shot six women, one of whom died from her injuries, after gaining access by taking a young girl hostage.

The list goes on. Whether church, synagogue, mosque, or temple, information on attacks at places of worship is easy to find. It's not our intent to detail every single attack, but rather to share some of the more significant incidents in recent memory. These few incidents out of many contain the lessons we need to learn to be better prepared both to prevent them and to respond should our best efforts fail.

Lessons from history

The incidents we chose represent turning points in the types of attacks on places of worship. One of those turning points is the increase in casualties over time.

Body count

The 1963 bombing of the 16th Street Baptist Church was an exclamation point on the racial tensions brewing in the United States at that time. The escalation of violence wasn't religious in nature, and the target wasn't picked because of the religion, but rather because of vicious racial hatred. The attack's location was chosen because it contained the most targets with the fewest obstacles in the way.

· · ·

The goal was body count — significant loss of life. Sadly, four beautiful young lives were taken during this attack and 22 others were injured. Despite that, and the use of a mass-casualty weapon, the carnage fell short of what the attackers desired.

It's useful to remember that the infamous Columbine High School massacre was intended to be a bombing. The two killers had a complex and involved attack planned, including a fire bomb to distract firefighters, as many as 99 improvised explosive devices (IEDs) to maximize casualties inside the school itself, propane tanks rigged with detonators to destroy the cafeteria, and car bombs outside the school to kill fleeing victims and first responders.

Luckily their bomb-making skills were not well developed. Had all of their devices successfully detonated, they may have killed as many as 400 people that day. Their original plan was to stay outside and shoot students who fled the bombs in the building, but because the bombs failed to go off, they were forced to enter the building to shoot students and staff.

The lesson for those of us who have taken on the responsibility of planning responses to these kinds of attacks is that the initial attack may only be diversionary. An escalation may be planned and there may be secondary attacks. We also need to prepare for the possibility that our attacker has a backup plan.

Targeted killings

In the 1974 shooting death of Alberta King, the killer made it clear whom he wanted to kill: "All Christians are my enemies," and black pastors were at the top of his enemies list. While he changed the person he originally intended to kill (King Sr.), his overall target never changed. The location and the individuals chosen were a function of their standing in the community. The intended results of the attack were press coverage and the spread of his ideology. (It's worth noting that, in some ways, his plan did work — he got the press coverage he wanted.)

The killing of specific people, particularly to advance a cause through news media coverage, is a component of many attacks over the last few decades. As the 24-hour news cycle has taken hold, the ability to become famous by killing others — particularly well-known others — is enough to motivate many attackers.

Collateral damage

Not all attacks on places of worship are political or the result of a specific ideology. The St. John Fellowship Baptist Church attack is a classic example of a domestic altercation spilling over into a place of worship. The targets were clearly the family: The attacker wanted to kill his wife and child. Unbeknownst to the people in that congregation, he had just come from killing his mother-in-law at her home a few blocks from the church.

As in other similar incidents, once his primary targets were killed, the attacker had no issue with killing others who just happened to be in the same place at the same time. It shows us something we would do well to remember: An attacker can quickly transition from killing his primary target to killing others with little to no prior planning.

Never underestimate the level of violence a domestic situation can present when it spills over into a place of worship. The attacker is likely to be very unstable, not at all concerned with his own life, and may even blame clergy or others in the congregation for the breakup of his relationship. If your congregation offers any kind of relationship counseling, be aware that you could eventually become a target of someone upset that his marriage is in trouble.

Shooting up the neighborhood

Sometimes, however, the target isn't specific and easily identified. Sometimes the target is whoever is in the general area when the attack occurs. These attacks seem to result in greater casualties — more injuries and deaths — as no one is passed over. Everyone in the area is a target.

For instance, although we may never know the full motive behind attack at the First Baptist Church in Sutherland Springs, it appears the target of the attack was simply the church itself — the entire congregation. Although there was some indication of a domestic disturbance, it appears that anyone attending church that day was a target. This is supported by the tactic of shooting at the church itself before entering and randomly killing parishioners.

We don't have to accept more attacks and mounting casualties. By studying the kinds of targets, some of the motivations of the attackers, and a clear identification of the threats we face, we can devise the tools necessary to adequately prepare for and reduce the number of casualties in future events.

What motivates attackers?

First, it's important to understand that those who target places of worship rarely hold their targets as sacred as we may. Many people have the perception that everyone is constrained by the same conscience or honor of the worship performed. Because they have the same honor, they'd never dare do anything that would disrupt or interfere. Right?

. . .

In reality, those who wish to do harm simply don't care about the morality, ethics, or laws that we do or in the ways that we do. In some cases, they specifically want to defy the rules of civilized society. The things that drive us to be decent and kind mean nothing to them; they're not driven by the same codes we are.

If you take nothing else from this discussion, understand that our perception may not be the reality they live in. The failure to understand this mismatch between what we believe and what they believe is one of the main reasons so many places of worship are vulnerable soft targets.

It's difficult to place ourselves in the position of another person where violent impulses are concerned. It's easy to empathize with someone who is coping with loss or other sadness, but almost impossible to do so with someone whose life is a continuous rage. It's even harder to see things from the standpoint of someone who wishes to cause pain and suffering for mere political ends — or even just for the thrill of the act itself.

While it may be nearly impossible to completely understand an attacker's motivation, we can understand that attackers do have motivation, that it is different than ours, and that they will see our pain and suffering very differently than we do. Accepting that evil exists and doesn't play by our rules is the first step to being able to protect ourselves from it.

Getting ahead of the curve

If we want safe places of worship, we must get ahead of those who wish to do us harm. Reactive security -- security focused on dealing with an incident as (or after) it happens -- is a model based on loss. It focuses not on prevention but on response only after an attack is recognized. Firearms training, for instance, is an example of reactive security.

When it comes to life — the lives of our members and fellow congregants — reactive security is, at a minimum, unacceptable. At worst, it is negligent to be on the reactive end of a response instead of on the proactive.

Know thy enemy

While watching for potential threats based on what happens to others, the reality is that threats change from place to place. Threats from opposing religious groups, for instance, are common in many parts of the world and are the largest concern to congregations in those areas. But in this country, they're probably not a realistic risk for you and your congregation.

In this book, we hope to show how important the concept of risk assessment is to the foundation of security in any place of worship. We'll show how important the constituent activities, such as active threat intelligence, are to a comprehensive security plan.

In the end, if we don't know our enemy or understand the threat they pose, we will never be prepared to meet those risks. Our shared goal, regardless of the religion of the members who meet in a place of worship, is to keep people safe while they worship

Once we realize how large a target our places of worship present, and the numerous vulnerabilities that exist in them, we can begin to address how to harden those targets and make them less appealing to the people who would do them harm.

. . .

**A personal account from Joshua: International incidents fore-
tell trouble at home**

On September 7, 2001, just days prior to the 9/11 attacks in the United
States, I watched as information came in about the Jos riots involving
Christians and Muslims in Jos, Nigeria. At the time, I had started
researching a book about church security (the one I didn't finish until
my co-author, with more experience than I have, led the way).

During that research, my attention was drawn to Africa and the
tensions among religious groups throughout the continent. During the
2001 Jos Riots, three Churches of Christ, the main Assemblies of God
church, an Apostolic Church, and several mosques were burned or
damaged. The ensuing ten days of riots left at least 1,000 people dead,
including some who were set on fire. Mass burials had to be arranged,
and the riots resulted in the displacement of thousands more people.

In the USA, our attention was diverted from what was going on as we
dealt with our own atrocities. The incidents in Nigeria and the attacks
on the World Trade Center were fresh in my mind when I attended a
post-9/11 lecture from a seasoned FBI Counter-Terrorism Agent. I've
never forgotten his words: "Watch what happens overseas. Our
enemies practice their tactics in other countries, then bring the
perfected versions to our homeland." His advice stuck with me over
the years, and I've watched carefully the violence in places of worship
overseas. I've contemplated how the same kind of violence could result
in similar damage closer to home, and there have been echoes of overseas incidents in the attacks we've seen here.

Importance of perspective

It's worth noting that active killer incidents, as newsworthy as they are, are of relatively low probability compared to the many other threats faced by people of faith. That doesn't mean we shouldn't prepare for attacks — we must — only that there are other things we need to prepare for as well.

For instance, medical emergencies happen far more frequently than mass attacks. Joshua has personally witnessed two deaths during or immediately after worship services, as well as nearly a dozen medical issues that required an ambulance response. Grant has seen heart attacks, multiple drug-intoxicated intruders, a diabetic seizure, and a severe bleeding injury resulting from broken glass on premises. They're important, too.

As it happens, the risk assessment and planning we'll do for the active killer will help us prepare for those other events as well. Conversely, the responses we put in place for a murderer will also be of value when the event is less sinister. Our model is that of "all risk," preparing for all types of plausible events that could occur at our places of worship.

WHAT'S AT RISK?

Not every environment or event needs exactly the same kind of security, but they all need to be considered when security planning is done. It's very easy, and very common, to focus on the major gatherings in the main worship areas to the exclusion of other places and events.

What follows is by no means a complete list, but rather a reminder of the people, places, and activities that need to be considered in any security plan. The security needs will likely be different: Sometimes the risk of outside attack may be high, while at other times attacks from the inside — by a member or person intimately familiar with the institution — are more likely. In some cases medical emergencies might be the most common danger, while everyone is at risk for environmental and natural disasters.

The security response may be as simple as doing fire-escape drills, and as complex as providing a first responder team (*a supervised and organized group who are trained to respond to various types of emergencies, from medical issues to active killer events.*) Each environment needs to be considered separately, and its unique security needs identified and addressed.

Where worshippers gather

Many faith communities have one modest building in which they gather, while larger communities may have a campus consisting of various facilities. Each building has its own common use and its own specific security issues.

When people begin thinking about security for their congregation, they immediately think of the main building — the church, synagogue, temple, or mosque itself. This is usually the biggest, most visible, and most easily accessed facility in any worship community, large or small. (We'll use the word "sanctuary" to refer to these structures, as it seems to be the most commonly accepted.)

The sanctuary often has multiple points of entry (and exit). It has risks for accident and disaster (think candles) that may not exist in other buildings. The sanctuary attracts and holds the largest number of people, increasing the likelihood of certain kinds of incidents.

In many cases, though, the sanctuary isn't the only building involved. Anywhere people gather in the name of the congregation needs to be considered and security resources properly budgeted.

The business of the congregation

The business office is often the place where people are present during non-worship hours. It's not unusual for larger congregations to have standard office hours and staff. The business office is a target not only for personal crime, but also for theft and financial crimes — even embezzlement.

The office is often where clergy is available to the community. It the place where they may do counseling and outreach. Because of this, the offices may attract angry or despondent people who might wish to harm themselves or others.

It's not uncommon for people whose marriages have failed to blame the people who attempted to counsel them during their difficulties. They may take out their aggressions when clergy is most available — during office hours. Those who feel rejected by the congregation may also take this path to act out their rage.

Drug and alcohol counseling is a common part of outreach at many congregations, and people under the influence are often irrational and unpredictable.

In these cases, it's not just the clergy who are at risk. Any support staff present may also become targets. The business office is often overlooked when security planning is done, and it shouldn't be.

The school

Many worship communities have schools as part of their operations. Some are in session only during worship, while others (especially in Catholic dioceses) operate full time and may include everything from infant day care through high school.

Schools of all kinds, both secular and religious, are notoriously soft targets. Attacks on schools often succeed, with horrifying results. This is because the open, trusting environment of education often works counter to what needs to be done to provide security.

Congregations that have large and well-regarded educational programs (again, this is often the case with parochial schools) face a double threat: Not only are they subject to the attacks specific to their religious nature, but also to the secular attacks from which public schools suffer.

If the congregation has a school, be it part time or full time, its students and staff must be protected just as well as the worshippers in the sanctuary.

Clergy housing

Whether referred to as a rectory, parsonage, presbytery, vicarage, manse, priory, pastorium, or just "house," the dwelling place of clergy may also be a target for attackers. It's usually no secret where clergy lives, particularly if the house is (as many are) located on the grounds of the institution. As a result, it may become the target of attack from angry or disaffected people.

Many of the issues with business offices also affect clergy housing. In fact, the de facto business office of many smaller congregations is the minister's/priest's/rabbi's house. Many members of the clergy do counseling in their house. As a result, the same security precautions we would apply to a separate business office also apply here.

If on the grounds, it may be the only building with clear activity after business or worship hours. Of course, any dwelling can be a target for thieves and burglars. Vows of poverty aside, it's still not pleasant to have one's belongings sifted through and stolen!

. . .

Special services and events

While the main sanctuary on the Sabbath is usually the focus of most security efforts, and the crowded services on holidays usually get increased attention, people are congregated in and around the facilities at many other times. These events provide opportunities for attacks, but are usually ignored in security planning. As a result, they present an easy opportunity for anyone who knows the habits of the congregation or has put effort into surveillance.

For example, many communities have some sort of evening religious education during the week; Wednesday evenings are very common in Christian churches here in the U.S. They are often well attended, presenting a tempting target for an attacker.

Funerals provide another gathering opportunity. The service for a well-respected member of the community will often have a very large attendance, providing opportunities for an attacker. Many people attending funerals are elderly, so medical emergencies are a major concern.

In the Catholic and some older Protestant traditions, the hearing of confessions is common. There have been attacks on priests during confession, and it's not unheard of for a penitent to become angry during the event. The priest and other participants may be at risk when this happens.

Many religious organizations offer group counseling for alcohol and narcotics addictions. A participant in the throes of withdrawal can become angry, either at themselves or other members of the group, and require physical intervention.

. . .

Numerous other special events and services should be considered in security planning. It's often easy to forget that many security threats apply to smaller or less important gatherings, but when security is provided in a place of worship, any gathering of people should be included. These smaller events may not need the same kind or extent of security, but everyone needs some sort of protection.

HOW SHOULD WE PREPARE?

Both of the authors have heard a joke about preparedness ascribed to both Christian and Jewish traditions. We have no doubt it exists, in some form, in every religion due to the universality of its message:

A man is at home enjoying a delicious meal. A knock is heard at the door, and there stands his neighbor with news that a flood is coming. The water is rising rapidly, emergency evacuation orders have been issued, and he should get out before it's too late.

The man waves the neighbor off and says, "God will provide!" The neighbor leaves for higher ground.

As the waters rise, the man is forced into the upstairs rooms to escape. Another neighbor comes floating by in a boat. The man sticks his head out the second-floor window and the neighbor tells him the water is rising even faster. He implores the man to get into the boat so they can get to safety.

Once again, the man waves the neighbor off by saying, "I'm not afraid. God will provide!" The neighbor starts up his outboard engine and, shaking his head, motors off to safety.

The waters do in fact keep rising, and the man is forced out onto the roof. A helicopter, searching for survivors, hovers over him as the crew yells for him to get into the basket so he can be hoisted into the helicopter and flown to safety.

Not surprisingly, the man yells back that he's not afraid of the flood, because "God will provide for me!"

The helicopter flies off and leaves the man on the roof, where he is finally overcome by the rising water.

After his death, the man appears before God to answer for his life, and he's none too happy about being there. He says, in exasperation, "I had faith in you! I was waiting for you to provide for me, to deliver me from the certain death of the flood! Why did you abandon me?"

God looks at the man and says, with a note of irritation, "I sent you a warning, a boat, and a helicopter — what more did you want?"

Leaving it all in God's hands?

Faith is, of course, the cornerstone of any religious community. At the same time, bad things happen to people regardless of the strength of their faith. We can't imagine a situation where, for instance, a house of worship wouldn't have a sprinkler system or fire alarm or fire extinguishers solely on the strength of their faith.

We don't turn off the sprinklers because we expect God to keep our buildings from burning down. We don't cancel our insurance in the belief that we are somehow immune from all harm. And yet, your authors have encountered situations where the security needs of a congregation were dismissed with a wave of the hand and a hearty "God will provide!"

We all understand what the man in our story doesn't: God isn't our babysitter. We have to be participants in our own protection. Our view is that he has, in fact, already provided everything we need — by giving us the intelligence, ability to learn, dedication, tools, moral compass, and the free will to keep ourselves and those around us safe from harm. How disrespectful would it be to refuse those gifts?

The moral imperative

Imagine a brand-new office or government building that didn't have fire alarms, proper wiring, emergency exits, lighted stairwells, or engineering for high winds, snow loads, or seismic events.

Most people would rightly wonder who was in charge of the building project and why he so cavalierly disregarded not only building codes and laws, but also the responsibility for the safety of the people who would use the structure.

Yet on a regular basis, we gather large numbers of people to worship in spaces that may not be up to current codes, without any plans for what should happen in case of a fire, a medical emergency, or even a mass-casualty attack. And no one seems to worry about that.

It's time we all did. Each of us, as members of worship communities, should be looking at the people gathered with us and ask, "What would we do if ..."

Of course not everyone will do that. Some won't see the need, and most won't even think about it because they assume someone else already has. The reality is that, in most worship communities, the safety and security of the members have been ignored.

Every worship community needs people to plan for their safety and security. It may start with a single concerned person motivating others to join the cause, but it takes more than an individual to do the entire job.

The task ahead

It seems simple enough, but the puzzle of congregational security has a lot of pieces. Not everyone is cut out for all of the tasks required; each individual will find tasks they like and those they don't. Some of the pieces in this process will seem boring, tedious, contentious, and even ugly to some people. Others will find them interesting, engaging, and energizing.

Everything starts with understanding

Everyone involved needs to face up to the realities of themselves, the other volunteers, the congregation, and the environment in which you all coexist.

Here is a good exercise for everyone who is part of the safety planning process. Before reading the rest of the book, each person should take 15 or 20 minutes and write down short answers to the following questions:

- Take stock of yourself: Why are you involved? What causes you to donate your time, talents, and energy to this cause? Do you have the motivation and dedication to see this project through?

- What about the other people who have come together to make your worship community safer and more resilient? Is it a group of friends, activity partners, or is it a coming together of interested and concerned congregants? What are their specific talents? Do they mirror yours, or do they complement each other? Are there gaps in the group's knowledge or skills? Did you come together spontaneously, or did someone ask you to become involved?

- What's your congregation like? Urban, suburban, rural? Is the congregation older, younger, or mixed? What percentage of members have children still at home? How would you describe the socioeconomic status of your membership? Do you have wide gaps in income and education, or is everyone of pretty equal accomplishment?

- What facilities are you trying to protect? Do you have a school, multiple buildings, or separate clergy housing? Do you often send kids on trips?

- How about your clergy? How involved will they be in this process? How would you describe their political positions — and are those positions radically different than the congregation or the local population? Are they very visible and active in local causes, or do they stay close to their members and not engage much with the outside community?

- Finally, what are your biggest security concerns? Where do you see dangerous gaps in your congregation's preparedness? What do you think is the most pressing concern — and what do you see as the best way to address that?

Even brief answers are useful. After everyone has answered all of the questions, compare notes. Each involved person will likely have a different perception of most of those questions. By seeing the issue through other's eyes, everyone will come away with a deeper understanding of the road ahead.

Planning - the key to success

This may come as a surprise, but security for a house of worship is really all about planning. The planning process involves identifying the potential targets, figuring out the threats those targets face, determining how the targets are vulnerable, and then coming up with ways to reduce the chances of actually facing a loss.

Security isn't about guns and practicing to shoot down terrorists. It is about knowing what's vulnerable, why it's vulnerable, and doing something about it. Sometimes the planning may include armed security teams, but other times (most of the time, in fact) something far less exciting is exactly what's needed. The planning process is where everyone learns what's needed.

Getting support

If you are that single concerned person, you'll need to rally others to your cause, others who feel the same moral responsibility you do and share your motivation to live your beliefs through real deeds. You'll need fellow congregants who are as motivated as you are to do something about the state of the community's preparedness.

Once a core group exists, the process can start. The group will investigate, identify risks and vulnerabilities, then make plans to shore up the weaknesses. Those plans will include prevention, response and recovery activities, perhaps identifying response teams to deal with incidents and provide for healing and rebuilding in the aftermath.

The overriding goal should be to make worship a safe and secure activity, one in which families and the elderly can participate with the confidence that someone has thought about their wellbeing and provided for it.

Yes, all this requires budgeting

We've never met anyone who admitted to enjoying making a budget, but it's an important part of security. There are always expenses, even with large amounts of volunteer labor, and some understanding of the budgeting process is important.

The most critical point on the subject of budgeting is to be honest. No one likes getting into the middle of a project only to find out there isn't enough money to finish it. As the group identifies what it believes necessary to mitigate the risks to the worship community, the estimates need to be as accurate as they can be.

Don't allow any one person's reticence to face financial issues set the group up for failure. There will always be people who won't face a money problem, dismiss financial concerns, or assume costs will be lower in order to sell the project to the keepers of the purse strings. It's better to scale back plans so they fit the budget rather than risk everything on the rocks of fiscal realities.

This is also true for the volunteer hours required to put the plan into place. One of the resources in an overall safety program will be available labor, both in the work of planning and in any actual response. Underestimating the amount of nature of the work involved, or overestimating volunteer enthusiasm, can sink a project just as surely as an empty bank account.

(We note that while most people recoil at the thought of preparing a budget, it's the rare worship community that doesn't have at least one accountant or business manager among its members. They're used to, and good at, the budgeting function and should be approached to help.)

. . .

Who does the work?

The work in putting together a comprehensive safety plan falls into three distinct functional categories:

- The **Steering Group** is responsible for the overall organization and groundwork — budgeting, decision-making, broad goals and rules. This is where the whole process starts and is overseen.
- The **Planning Group** is responsible for the work of identifying targets, threats, and vulnerabilities. They are the ones who put together the mitigation plan: what needs to be done, by whom, and when. This is where the majority of the hard work of mitigation planning is done.
- The **First Responder Team (FRT)** is the "boots on the ground" of the safety program. Whether they handle security, disaster response, or medical intervention, these are the people who actually carry out the mitigation plans. They are also the public face of the process, and there may be more than one.

These three functional groups are collectively referred to as the **Safety Council**, though each has a unique, important, and equal role in providing for the safety and security of everyone in the congregation.

In a large congregation with many available volunteers, these groups may be broken down into smaller committees, each charged with a specific task. For instance, the Planning Group may have individual committees for Target Assessment, Threat Assessment, and so on; the Steering Group may have a separate Budget Committee.

In smaller communities, these functional tasks may be allocated differently or the Planning and Steering Groups collapsed into a single entity. In very small congregations, the same group of people may be called upon to shoulder all of the functions.

. . .

The work to be done, however, remains roughly the same.

In any case, some provision must be made for overseeing the actions of any First Responders acting on behalf of the congregation. We'll talk more about this in a later chapter, but here it's sufficient to emphasize that regardless of the size of the community, response and review functions always need to be separated in some way.

Everyone can contribute

Safety and security aren't just the job of a specialized team. There will be things that everyone in the congregation can do, and figuring out where everyone can contribute is a great way to get the membership to support a safety plan.

Certain tasks should always be left to a First Responder Team. Other tasks can be done by most people in most congregations. Some action items may be best handled by the clergy, some call for a specific gender of volunteer, and others should probably be left to professionals.

Some things even kids can do!

This is why taking stock of what the congregation is like is so important. Knowing who the members are and what they can do will help guide the Safety Council in assigning tasks and responsibilities. As plans start to come together, everyone should be thinking about the tasks to be done and if some of them can involve people who are not officially part of the Council.

. . .

It's likely that more people can be gainfully involved than anyone initially believed.

The training requirement

Beyond the formal, trained First Responder Team, there are many responses that may (and in many cases should) involve other members of the community. For them, some amount of training will be necessary. Even when a response is being led by a First Responder Team, those they serve may need to be taught what to do under specific circumstances.

Along with that training must come occasional practice to maintain the skills.

Skills like minor first aid and performing CPR are ones that every congregation needs, but very few ever make such training available to their members. Even basic life-saving trauma response, which many wrongly assume to need highly skilled professionals, can be easily learned in an afternoon.

(As this is being written, one of the authors is listening to local fire department radio traffic. A member of a nearby church is suffering a heart attack during services, and from what the dispatcher is telling paramedics, the patient isn't being attended to by anyone. This type of medical emergency happens frequently, but surprisingly few congregations are prepared for it.)

If it's decided that armed security will be part of the First Responder Team's duties, they'll need specific training in the unique demands of shooting around other people in crowded areas — and they'll need regular, structured range time to practice those very perishable skills.

· · ·

Training also means such mundane things as fire drills for the children in religious study classes. They need to know what to do in case of fire (or tornado or earthquake, depending on the local dangers) just as they do in their regular school.

Even the adults may need to be trained which exits to use and where to go once clear of the building. Does everyone know where the fire extinguishers are and how to use them? You might be surprised how many people answer "no" to both of those questions.

There are many such opportunities for congregational education and practice. Make room in the planning process for the necessary training sessions, and for occasional drills to keep the skills in usable condition.

WHY RELIGIOUS SPACES ARE HARD TO SECURE

Putting institutional security into place is never without issue. However, places of worship have unique obstacles that are not present in any other environment. Unique attitudes toward faith, worry, planning, and pacifism become big factors in the difficulty of securing places of worship.

How big and difficult these obstacles have become is illustrated in the writing of this book.

Attitudes of faith, pacifism, and resignation

Both authors agreed from the beginning that this book should not cater to any specific religion. We both believe that, regardless of any religious differences, the safety and security of human lives transcend religion. We also wanted to stay away from controversial religious debates and stick to how we can properly secure our places of worship.

. . .

However, as Josh wrote his portion of this very section, he struggled at times with his message. It was, for him, the most difficult portion of this book. He couldn't help remembering the many religious debates he's had with people over safety and security. Many of these debates were among members of his own religious community.

Such debates are not unique to any one religious tradition. Grant remembers meetings where congregational safety was debated and where the very notion of security was questioned because of the impact on religious tradition — the implication being that paying attention to any kind of security violated religious practices. "God will provide!"

Through their personal debates, the authors have come to accept the fact that some people will never see the need for safety and security in their private lives, let alone in their communal ones. They will use arguments of faith, worry, pacifism, and logistics, among others, to justify their view against the need for safety and security for themselves or their families.

We don't want to get into the details of each of those obstacles, because they vary with the specific religious tradition (and sometimes even between movements or denominations inside each tradition), but it's a sure bet we've all heard the arguments[1].

Although we personally cannot see how these mistaken beliefs can be held without being hypocritical, it's possible some may have done so successfully. If they desire to live their private lives with those obstacles in place for themselves, we both honor them for their commitment. In fact, we support their right to live by their own beliefs and make every effort not to be a stumbling block for them.

. . .

At the same time, those of us who do take responsibility for our safety and that of those around us must expect the same in return. When others want to bring their opposing beliefs into the public environment — the congregational space — and become obstacles to our safety and security (and that of our families), conflicts will occur.

These self-imposed obstacles to security should not be allowed to infringe on the moral responsibility our places of worship have to ensure the safety and security of everyone who comes to participate. It is essential that these obstacles be dealt with as purely personal issues that need to remain outside our places of worship.

We present soft targets

Places of worship are traditionally soft targets by design. They are by nature open environments where people are welcomed with outstretched arms. They bring people together frequently and at predictable times. The very existence of a place of worship is defined by the ability to let all people who wish to worship do so, and to encourage new people to come and join the community. As communities we want — or, more specifically, we *need* — them to be open environments where people can freely come and go.

The very things that enable places of worship to exist, though, are the same things that make them hard to secure.

Institutional inertia

It seems when a place of worship has been a soft target for so long, that status becomes part of the tradition of the institution. It becomes so entwined into the institutional memory that, in order to change, it requires a wholesale upending of the institutional mindset. This includes an acceptance of the breaking of tradition, which is not easy in an environment where everything is a tradition!

Any newlywed who's had to break a holiday tradition to be with the new spouse's family can relate to how difficult that can be. It's hard to pull people away from what they have spent decades doing.

But do we have to accept that places of worship are always going to be soft targets, and leave it at that? We submit that, with a little effort, we can make our places of worship open and inviting while still reducing the vulnerabilities they face.

But we may have to "bend" just a little on how we traditionally approach the idea of an open and inviting environment. Take, for example, the usher who is posted at the main door during worship. This person can represent the desired open and inviting environment while still being able to control access to the building if a threat presents itself.

Yes, we acknowledge it may be difficult to overcome some of the objections from more traditional or conservative congregants, but it's not impossible. Solutions exist that provide a balance between presenting an inviting environment and still allowing us to address safety and security issues.

Budgetary concerns

One of the most persistent objections to securing places of worship is, of all things, money. Sadly, this one obstacle has halted many congregations from implementing safety and security plans their volunteers have put together. Anyone reading this book will no doubt have seen this dynamic at work as well.

. . .

The most amazing thing is that these budgetary concerns seem to rise and fall with the news cycle. Let's look at a fictional example that has all the components we've seen in a range of actual situations.

An active killer event occurs somewhere in the world. It doesn't even need to be a house of worship, just another soft target where multiple people are killed by an attacker (or attackers). News outlets instantly notify the world and, before the victims' bodies are cold, every firearms instructor, retired law enforcement officer, martial arts instructor, and gun collector instantly become church security and "active shooter" experts.

At the same time, people are scared whenever they go anywhere — like a house of worship — with large numbers of people present. Some can't face their fears and stop showing up. They look to their clergy and congregational leadership to reassure them and keep them safe.

That same leadership knows they are not doing what needs to be done to allay the fears, so they appease the congregation by announcing they are looking for an expert who can help ease the minds of the members. The self-proclaimed experts, their reputations bolstered by appearances on local news channels, agree to come up with a class on how to handle an active shooter. They promise to teach members of the congregation some skills, often involving learning how to shoot, so they can protect their fellow congregants.

The fact that they offer it to the congregation for free — perhaps even including handouts and ammunition in their donation — makes it an attractive option for the people who handle the congregational budget.

And it makes the experts feel good that they're doing something to "help."

The promised free class takes place, and half the people who signed up for the class don't show up. Perhaps one or two members of the congregational leadership attend. At the end of the course, everyone is excited and feels like real progress is being made. A week passes, and maybe one or two small things that take little effort or money are implemented.

Any talk of further effort to enhance security, or to actually spend money, is met with the reminder that the problem has already been addressed by the free class. If members of the congregation insist, perhaps forming a committee to look further into the matter, the leadership responds with a non-committal "put together a proposal for us." What they mean, in fact, is "we're hoping you won't go to the effort to put this together. If you do, though, we'll kill it by not having the necessary funding."

Several months later, the whole sequence of events is a distant memory. Then another incident occurs and shakes up the members, and the process starts all over again.

You're not the first

Why can we relate this in such detail? Because we've watched this play out the same way in our own congregations, and in those we've been asked to help — in different religious groups and different places of worship. And objections almost always come down to money.

From what we've both seen, money is one of the most significant issues in securing places of worship. The same congregation that will spend $20,000 to pave the parking lot won't spend $200 to keep their 150 members safe. We've seen it happen more than once.

Ironically, security — real security — doesn't necessarily cost a lot of money. Most security solutions are actually inexpensive. Perhaps you've heard of the Pareto Principle: 80% of results come from 20% of the resources spent. Any congregation can achieve dramatic increases in their security (the 80%) without spending huge sums of money (the 20%).

But without a commitment to spending the modest amount of money necessary, progress won't happen. There has to be a commitment to funding the efforts, no matter how modest they are.

We've observed that congregational leadership will never take classes and security recommendations seriously until they're on the hook for the money — and the amount of money is immaterial. Be very clear what we mean: It's not the money itself, but rather the *commitment* the money represents that is important.

How to get past the money objection

We've independently approached this issue in a surprisingly similar manner: We confront the undecided, those who present the impediment to progress, at the very beginning and challenge them to commit in writing to a security budget, no matter how modest. If they won't, we won't waste their time and ours working on solutions that will never be embraced by the leadership. Without commitment, it's all talk — and actual security requires action.

. . .

As the coming generations mature, we believe that safety and security during worship will be much bigger concerns for them. They're the ones growing up in the increasingly dangerous world, where attacks on large groups are becoming less surprising. Institutions that don't take the security of their members seriously, and don't budget time and money appropriately, may lose membership. Some may even disappear.

Don't let money be the obstacle that keeps your place of worship from being safe to attend. Determine what the congregation can honestly afford to spend, then make an appropriate and balanced plan that provides the most security possible.

Why we need to change

According to research we did in writing this book, there is a massive and ongoing decrease in people attending worship services across all religions. One study indicated that only 28% of adults between the ages of 23 and 37 attend religious services. This is down from 52% in previous generations. The number one conclusion of multiple researchers is that religious institutions are having a hard time changing with the needs of this younger generation.

It's worth pointing out that the Millennial generation places a higher value on safety than any other generation — followed closely by GenX. During their formative years, they watched mass school shootings change the way they went to school. The nuclear bomb drills their grandparents endured were replaced with active shooter drills.

Those who were born at the end of the 1980s grew up in a world where terrorism in their own backyards was a legitimate fear. They also grew up going through checkpoints and being scanned for weapons before entering schools and other buildings where large numbers of people were grouped together.

. . .

While some insist on living in the past, the reality is that times are changing. More people are concerned about their safety and security than ever before. It's no coincidence that attendance numbers are down in places where large groups of people gather and where little to no security is in place. Younger generations weigh risk/reward more than any others, and may decide the risk isn't worth taking. These generations are telling us what they need, but few seem to be listening.

It's time for places of worship to address the safety and security of their congregants, before there's nothing left to secure. We need to change because it's important to the survival of our traditions and communities.

But to do that, we also need to stop looking at security measures through the eyes of past generations, which had a bigger risk appetite from years of the Cold War and its constant false alarms. They got used to tolerating risk, because nothing ever really happened.

The new generations don't have that risk tolerance. They've seen actual attacks happen, again and again, and don't want to be victims themselves. They want security and aren't getting it. We contend that houses of worship are seeing the results of not providing for the real needs of their communities — and it's time to change.

Respecting religious traditions

We touched on the idea of how religious traditions can be obstacles when putting safety and security plans in place. We also hinted at how balance is needed.

. . .

Each religion is unique. Traditions date back centuries, sometimes even millennia, and many sects and denominations hold, to the best of their ability, to those traditions. That being said, some are more willing than others to adapt those traditions to modern safety and security realities.

Some groups will always be less inclined to change, and we respect that. Our goal is to help those who sincerely ask for input, at the same time that we respect the doctrine and traditions of the group.

Notice we didn't say individuals' views. This is a very important distinction: We respect the doctrine and traditions of the group, even as we may disagree with the personal views of those who resist the work that needs to be done.

We believe this respectful approach goes a long way to easing the minds of the skeptical. When we can help put into place security measures that are virtually invisible to the rest of the community and still allow them to honor their traditions, trust is built between everyone involved.

One of the biggest fears of many leaders and members is intrusive or distracting security measures. They fear there will be so much security that it will conflict with their worship and destroy the atmosphere of a warm and inviting place for worship. We must be careful to balance what needs to be done to protect the people and what needs to be done to protect the sanctity of the worship.

This is why we are staunch promoters of covert security practices in most places of worship. With the exception of those who have already embraced an overt security presence, a covert approach allows security programs to exist where they otherwise would not have existed.

To get past these obstacles and make our places of worship more secure, we must be willing to give a little. It's all about balance. Respecting traditions is a good place to start.

WHY DO WE NEED FORMAL RISK MANAGEMENT?

When teaching workshops for places of worship, and being in charge of facility security ourselves, we've noticed the basis of many safety and security plans is nothing more than an undefined feeling that some kind of protection is needed. Very often one person (or perhaps a few people at most) have decided the congregation needs a specific kind of security, without regard to whether or not a plausible risk exists. More often than not, these security procedures are oriented toward a type of incident that isn't very likely.

We see this most commonly after an active killer incident, particularly a school shooting, has made national news. After those events, we often notice what can only be termed a militarization of places of worship. Often initiated by the firearm or tactical training hobbyists in the congregation, "security teams" carrying full-sized firearms, backup guns, and belts full of "security gear" appear. Random security implementations begin. Time, and very often money, are haphazardly thrown at the perceived problem until it feels like something has been done.

. . .

Sometimes it's surprising how far these fantasies go. Once a small investment has been made, expensive upgrades start being discussed: armored podiums, bullet-resistant vests, thermal cameras (of the type usually only carried by SWAT teams), and so on. Of course someone can't have all that cool tactical gear without the training to go with it, and so they'll start looking for shooting instructors who specialize in "worship tactical teams." Somehow these plans get leaked and discussed on the local television news, and people feel good that they're "doing something."

What usually happens is, once the immediacy of the perceived danger passes, the plans and training are never finished, and everything goes back to the way it was before — with no real progress made in respect to mitigating the very real risks faced by the institution.

Don't plan on feelings — or fears

Why does this cycle repeat itself all over the country? Because the people who implement these schemes base their activities on little more than feelings. There is nothing to logically justify their plans once the feelings subside.

What's more, not everyone feels the same way about security. When emotions are at the center of planning, the people who don't feel the same urgency dismiss them. Dissent arises and subtle resentment — at both the time and money spent — can result in a political fight that torpedoes later attempts at real security.

There are times when feelings are a good basis for individual decision-making. When the safety of many people is on the line, however, the feelings of one person (or even a few people) aren't enough. Objective analysis and planning are the only responsible ways to approach the problem.

. . .

Risk management is the tool to change from feelings to reason, from fear to resolve. Taking the time to determine what things are most likely to occur, and balancing them against the impact of those events supplies the logic-based justification for real security. This procedure, called assessment, is all about "showing your work" so that others can not only become part of the process and support it, but also help spot vulnerabilities that one (or even a few) might miss.

The more thoroughly the congregation performs the assessment process, the better they can explain and justify every bit of time and money spent to ensure the safety of their place of worship. However, unless the congregation is unusually small, not everyone can be involved. It's also not something any one person can do by themselves; a committee is needed to tackle this project.

The Planning Group

Another committee? Aren't most congregations already filled to the brim with committees? That may be true, but this one has a very specific job to do.

As noted earlier, feelings are a very bad way to make security decisions, and one person can't realistically do the topic any justice. There are a lot of pieces to consider, and a lot of work to be done. That requires a team effort, and that team is the Planning Group.

If there are not enough people on the Safety Council to staff a separate Planning Group, these tasks may be done by the whole Council — but they have to be done.

. . .

What tasks will the Planning Group perform?

The first and most important task is to go through the risk management process: to determine what's at risk (targets), what is putting them in danger (threats), where they might be vulnerable, how they should be secured, and finally putting into place the plans and procedures to enable the new security posture. This is a very large amount of work, requiring clear thinking and analysis.

If the Planning Group decides an active safety group (a First Responder Team, or FRT) is appropriate for the congregation, the Group may also serve in a supervisory role to the team(s). It's important for any active safety personnel to have proper oversight, as the potential for abuse of perceived authority is always a concern. This is especially true if any members of the FRT are allowed or authorized to be armed.

Who should be on it?

A large congregation will likely be composed of many different demographic groups (constituencies), and it's best if there is a representative of each in the Planning Group. Some constituent groups may have concerns that others don't, or be more vulnerable to some threats than others. Since the task of the Group will be to ensure the safety and security of the worship community as a whole, leaving one constituency out of the planning procedure damages the integrity of the process.

Seek out concerned, intelligent, trustworthy members from all the demographic groups in the worship community. Those people need to share a concern for the safety and security of everyone — not just those in their personal clique but in the community as a whole.

. . .

How many people?

The size of the Planning Group should reflect the size and composition of the congregation. The Group will get better information and make better decisions if they have a broad perspective on the concerns of the congregation. For that, more people are needed.

At the minimum, for a very small congregation, we suggest three people. When congregation numbers get into the thousands, a group of a dozen is not out of the question. If there are sufficient participants, the Planning Group might be subdivided to more efficiently handle specific tasks. One sub-group may focus on just threat assessment, while another may focus only on mitigation planning. They would report their findings to the Group for decision and perhaps transfer to another sub-group.

At some point, the rest of the congregation will need to be convinced about both the process and the result. Additional volunteers may be needed to staff the First Responder Team(s), or special financing may be needed to complete purchases. The more people who have been involved in the process, and the more representative of the congregation they are, the easier it will be to convince the whole community that what's been done is both necessary and appropriate.

The role of clergy

At some point the clergy needs to be involved in the process. Not only might they be a primary target themselves, but they also have a moral responsibility to see to the safety of their community. In addition, there may be doctrinal or observance issues with some types of security planning, and having their input may be critical to respecting religious tradition.

. . .

Ideally, they would be actively be involved from the beginning as a member of the Planning Group. That being said, in many congregations, clergy is already stretched thin with their regular duties, and they may simply not have time to appear at yet another meeting. This is particularly true in smaller congregations. If that's the case, having a religiously knowledgeable lay member who can serve as a liaison to the clergy may be a good compromise.

At the very least, make sure the religious leadership is not hostile to the idea of improving the congregation's security. If they aren't in agreement, it's quite likely that even the most well-intentioned and innocuous plans will be stillborn.

The importance of discretion

Members of the Planning Group need to be honest, trustworthy, and know how to keep their mouths shut. They'll be dealing with sensitive topics and material, the kinds of things that shouldn't be indiscriminately broadcast to the whole community. In some cases, damaging personal information may be encountered, and it's the committee's responsibility to ensure privacy is maintained.

This cannot be overemphasized: All members of the committee need to be able to trust each other, and the congregation at large needs to be able to trust the committee as a whole. Without that trust, there cannot be effective security and a warm, inviting congregation.

WHAT IS RISK MANAGEMENT?

Risk and danger are two words often used interchangeably, but in our world, they mean two very different things. Danger refers to anything that has the ability to do harm. Dangers can be natural, man-made, or even man himself. They present a threat, a perception or implication that harm may occur from a specific source.

Risk, on the other hand, is the likelihood of harm. Risk is the possibility of the danger actually happening, causing damage. We work to reduce the likelihood of things happening to us. In more precise terms, we work to mitigate risk to our worship communities.

This practice and process of mitigating risk is broadly referred to as risk management. It's both a process and an activity, encompassing planning, identification, evaluation, prioritization, and response to threats. It's the entire process of dealing with dangers to our lives, the lives of others, and our worship communities.

. . .

A different approach to risk management

In simple terms, the goal of risk management is to reduce our exposure to the possibility of loss. As it happens, there are a variety of ways to accomplish this goal. The one we use, and believe to be the most applicable to houses of worship, is called Target-Based Risk Management (TBRM).

This method is the result of decades of experience by both authors. Through trial and error, we've each learned to adapt traditional risk management practices — originally intended for natural disasters or executive protection — to the unique needs of worship communities. The results have been combined into what we're presenting here.

We're sharing this information because, in the end, we can only teach these topics face-to-face to a limited number of people. We hope our readers take the information in this book and use it to create hard targets within their own places of worship.

Wherever possible, we've stuck with the best practices of traditional risk management, and only vary from them in situations where we feel a strict clinical approach would limit our reader's ability to implement these concepts on their own. As we discovered when we began our collaboration, it was very easy to overwhelm those new to these concepts, making it impossible to "see the forest for the trees"!

We've distilled our approach to the most essential points, in order to make them easy to put into practice, even if someone is new to the very idea of risk management. We'll lay out the tools and the process, explain how to use them, and present a guide to doing so in worship communities of all kinds.

. . .

We also believe in a balance among degree of protection, use of resources, and ease of implementation. The tools used, the order in which the tasks are done, and the perspective used when deciding mitigation strategies are all factors in this delicate balance. This section is about helping people understand the tools and how to use them in balance to achieve an optimal degree of protection for their own worship community.

Pre-planning is critical

Before the actual activities of Target-Based Risk Management can begin, a foundation must be laid. It's very easy to jump ahead of the community's ability, interest, or even tolerance and end up with nothing to show for the effort. This pre-planning can (and should) be done even before the formal organizational framework has been established. It should involve everyone who's been recruited to serve on the Safety Council, even if the Steering Group, Planning Group, and First Responder Team have yet to be formed.

Don't skimp in these pre-planning activities. It's very common for people to skip this groundwork, only to find out later that there's no community agreement, no money, and no people to help. We strongly recommend that the following be reduced to writing, so that everyone has a document of agreement to which they can refer.

Start by getting the consent of both clergy and lay leadership. It's important that they be understanding of the need for better security and supportive of the efforts to secure their worship community. It's also important that the people involved understand and abide by any doctrinal or denominational restrictions on the safety/security activities.

Once that's been done, identify the available resources. Who will be involved? Is there a formal safety organization, or just a small group of people who share an interest in security topics? Who can be called upon to be part of the process? Does this effort have the support of both clergy and lay leadership? Who is likely to be hostile to this project, and what are their probable objections?

While much of the Target-Based Risk Management process is free, as the process progresses it's very likely (even certain) that certain items can only be addressed by spending money. Is the Finance Committee supportive of the safety initiative? What funds are immediately available to support the process? Are there people in the worship community who might be persuaded to help by donating resources? Can special fundraising events be held?

Finally, what is the time frame? Is this urgent because of a recent event or newly perceived threat, or can the Safety Council take the necessary time to fully address all the issues?

What is the Council responsible for?

The next step is to come to a clear understanding of the responsibilities and limitations of the group. In general, these can be classified as internal to the congregation and external to it.

By "internal," we mean those things that happen inside the worship community or on the property/in the facilities. They are things that are, to some extent, under the congregation's control and for which the internal safety/security procedures can mount an effective initial defense.

For instance, it would certainly be within the Council's purview to maintain security over thefts from offices, investigate those that happen, and present the findings to the police. It probably wouldn't be the Council's job to arrest the persons responsible, and certainly not to put them on trial, sentence, and jail them.

Will the First Responder Team be responsible for initial emergency medical response, or will they rely on the fire department for those things? If physical security is part of the overall safety plan, will the First Responder Team be charged with that and be active during worship activities, or will that task be delegated to a private security company?

How about fire suppression? Information security? Will the Safety Council be responsible for security only during worship services, or all week? Will their plans cover just the sanctuary, or the whole building? How about the grounds? And who deals with security for off-campus clergy dwellings?

Everyone involved in this pre-planning step should write down exactly what types of incidents, time frames, physical locations, and people they expect the Council be responsible for. That list will be the hard limits, the lines inside which the process of TBRM will be performed.

The basics of Target-Based Risk Management

As we said, there are many different ways to deal with risk. In this book, we focus on Target-Based Risk Management, which we believe is both most appropriate for houses of worship and easiest for the non-expert to grasp and utilize.

The word "target" refers to the people, facilities, and activities that may be at risk from any specific threat. They're the things the need protection, and the reason for the existence of the safety initiative in the first place. They are where resources and activities are focused.

Everything that surrounds or interacts with any target has an impact on its safety, either good or bad. The path to protection is to evaluate the current state of the target and make its future expected state more good than bad.

The TBRM process isn't as complex as it might seem. It consists of simple steps:

1. **Target Assessment:** Identify the likely targets — what needs protection and why?
2. **Threat Assessment:** Determine the specific dangers those targets might face.
3. **Vulnerability Assessment:** Where are the weaknesses that allow the threats to exploit the targets?
4. **Risk Assessment:** Assign a value to the combinations of Target, Threat, and Vulnerability to guide the planning.
5. **Mitigation Planning:** For each target, decide the best way to protect it from the identified threats.

This sounds like a complex procedure, but it's simply defining what the hazards (threats) are, determining just how susceptible the congregation is to them, and then doing something about the identified weaknesses. When each of those steps has been diligently performed, the result is an actionable plan that can begin to be put into place.

For the people who don't live in the risk management world every day, this simple process helps to focus thinking. It gives a way to think through the risks logically and provides the mindset necessary to successfully protect the house of worship. TBRM takes into account all the pieces necessary to successful defense: figuring out where the attack is likely to happen, what the objective of the attacker is, and how to defend against them.

The following chapters explain these steps in detail. At each step it's important to remember that danger doesn't come just from robbers or mass killers: Natural disasters such as tornados and earthquakes, along with man-caused disasters like fires and chemical spills, present deadly threats to a congregation as well. Don't neglect them in the planning process!

TARGET ASSESSMENT

Without knowing what needs protection and why, it's impossible to have any kind of security plan. The first step in risk management, then, is to identify what the likely targets are.

What's a target?

It's easy to think of targets as they relate to criminal activity; the criminal targets people or things for theft or destruction. But as we use the term, a target can be a building at risk from fires, tornadoes, or earthquakes; a target can also be a person with a medical condition at risk of a heart attack.

The term "target," then, means any identifiable thing that's at risk from any identifiable danger. Another way to think about targets is that they are the people, places, and things that the safety and security plan is expected to cover in some way.

This is a critical step because it's all too easy to throw personnel, equipment, and procedures at a perceived lack of safety or security, and end up not protecting the most important assets. Identifying the targets focuses the safety planning on what's most important: the things that need security from threats.

1. *The brainstorming approach*

In TBRM workshops, we gather around a whiteboard to do this step. We ask the participants to list anything at, in, or around their place of worship that might be the target of a thief or violent criminal.

These lists typically end up looking something like this:

- Our building
- Financial information
- Cash
- People
- Congregant information
- Electronic equipment
- Vehicles & personal property

It seems pretty comprehensive, doesn't it? This is just the start. From here we ask the participants to drill down further to specifics.

For example, the first item on a lot of lists is the building. We ask the students to think about what makes the building a target, e.g., which particular areas of the building are most likely to attract a thief? One answer might be the office where they put collections at the end of a worship service.

But it's not the office that's the primary target, is it? The target is really the money. The path the thief takes, through the building, is certainly at risk as a secondary target, but it's the money the thief is going for — and what, ultimately, needs to be protected.

Of course, in some cases the building might be the target in and of itself. Someone with an axe to grind with the congregation, such as a disaffected member, or someone who simply doesn't like the specific religion the building represents, might try to burn the building down. That makes the building the primary target.

It's important to be clear about what's at risk in order to protect it.

Direct and indirect targets

Whether a target is direct or indirect depends on perspective. If the threat impacts a specific person, if that person feels a need to protect himself, that person is a direct target. He may not be the primary target from the threat's point of view, but from his perspective that doesn't matter.

Let's use an over-the-top example: A nuclear missile fired by a hostile country at a military installation 15 miles from town is aimed at destroying a military target. The houses in between are simply collateral damage. Yet from the homeowner's standpoint, they are a direct target because the missile would kill them and the family. If someone actually faced such a threat, it would be prudent to build some sort of bunker to protect themselves.

The actions of the threat, whether it's a thinking, calculating human being or an indiscriminate source such as a hurricane, might be beyond the control of anyone in the worship community. Looking at the threat from the perspective of the target, though, will indicate whether preparations to deal with that threat should (or even could) be made.

. . .

The threat's point of view

A truly comprehensive risk management plan looks at a wide range of threats. It's sometimes referred to as "all-hazards planning," because the end goal is to minimize losses from whatever source.

The problem is that a true all-hazards approach is very resource intensive. To develop one requires a huge amount of work; to implement one requires a correspondingly large amount of money.

This is why we've adopted the TBRM approach. By limiting the scope of planning to the most important identified targets and the most plausible events, we can make the best use of always limited resources. Learning how an active threat looks at a target helps us understand why we might be chosen for attack, and also gives clues about how to protect from that attack.

Accidents and disasters are indiscriminate

Thinking about targets subject to natural disasters, medical emergencies, and predictable accidents is relatively straightforward. If an area has tornadoes but not earthquakes, it's easy to conclude which needs to be considered in the planning process. The methods of mitigation, response, and recovery for those types of threats are all defined and known beforehand.

Most natural disasters are indiscriminate. A forest fire targets everything in the countryside that can burn. A home that happens to be in the area is in danger, despite not being the sole target.

. . .

Identifying the target of a human attacker is more complex. Knowing what the targets are and how the attack might proceed requires getting into the head of an attacker.

The return on investment of an attack

Except for those relatively uncommon random incidents by mentally deranged individuals, targets usually have a return on investment (ROI) for the attacker. In other words, the attacker expects to get something in return for his efforts in planning and executing the attack.

What he gets doesn't necessarily need to be tangible, and in many cases isn't. Instead of money or jewelry, the reward he seeks might be notoriety, revenge, political upheaval, or simply a feeling of power and control over the victims. The major concern in his mind will be: Is the reward worth the risk of capture — or even just being deterred and denied a prize?

An attacker, whether he knows he's doing it or not, will almost always make some kind of risk/reward calculation in his decision of what and how to attack. A suicide attacker, for instance, doesn't normally want to kill just one person. He wants to kill as many as he can, so that the expenditure of his life has a net gain in his mind.

It's an admittedly grisly way of looking at a situation, but it's important because increasing the risk to the attacker — either through capture, injury, or simply being denied a sufficient return — serves deterrent and mitigation functions. It's not possible to do those things without understanding what he expects to gain.

Considering those things or individuals an attacker might target in the worship community, consider the effort they have to invest to get their expected return. To do this, it's helpful to think in terms of the attacker's anticipated reward.

This is different than his motivation.

The attacker's reasoning is a factor

An attacker may be mad at "Christian ideology" and decide to express his anger at religion by attempting to shoot people attending Sunday morning prayer services. His main goal might be to harm religion, to get back at the institution of worship, but his reward (success/failure) is measured by body count. He achieves his goal by killing people, and the more he kills, the greater his return on investment.

We've seen in past attacks that racism can be a motivation, manifested by a lethal attack on worshippers whose ethnicity differs from the attacker. Politics is always a flashpoint for violence, as are social issues. The more visible and the more outspoken any group or individual is, the more likely it is that someone will disagree with them — perhaps to the point of violence.

We are not saying any worship community should hide itself in fear, or abandon its outreach and educational efforts or its social positions. Rather, the people charged with protecting the congregation should understand why those activities might make them a target and think in terms of how someone might take out his anger on the community.

Targeting is a process, not an event

The important takeaway from this discussion is that, when dealing with human attackers, targeting is a process. The attacker will not drive by and suddenly think about turning into the parking lot to stage an attack. Attacks on houses of worship are seldom spur-of-the-moment decisions.

Instead, the attacker selects and classifies his target(s). As we suggested earlier, this may be a conscious or subconscious procedure. Whether the attacker knows he's doing it or not, he's sizing up the potential targets and figuring out which one will give him the best return for the least risk.

Location figures into this selection process as well. We don't mean to be simplistic, but the farther the distance to a target, the less likely the attacker seems to be to choose it. As long as there are other targets closer by that meet his motivations and have a favorable risk-to-return ratio, the attacker is likely to pick one of those over the one he has to travel to.

(This may be simply because the farther he has to travel, the greater the chance of discovery. The more time on the road, the more chance he might be pulled over for a traffic violation and found out. Whatever the reason, distance seems to be a deterrent in many cases.)

The times when the distance-equals-safety rule fails is when a particular congregation is chosen for a particular reason. The angry ex-husband may travel a long distance to seek revenge on his ex-wife's church, for example.

Neither of the authors believes targets are randomly chosen. After studying many attacks over a long span of time, we've come to the firm conclusion that an attacker's biases, beliefs, and prejudices dictate the targets. Further, there is always some kind of analysis — however hasty

— that has specific characteristics. It's those characteristics that might help you detect an attack before it happens.

It doesn't take long to come up with a good list of primary and secondary targets. Luckily, this process is both straightforward and only occasional. For most congregations, the targets don't change a lot over time. Once that list is made, it's time to figure out what those targets need protection from.

THREAT ASSESSMENT

Once the targets — those things or people who need protection — have been identified, the next step in the risk management process is to figure out what presents a threat to them.

What do we mean by "threat"?

A threat is an active and proximate danger that might damage or destroy a target; it poses the possibility of death or loss. Protecting targets from threats is the whole point of risk management.

A threat isn't necessarily a human being. Natural events can lead to property destruction or death just as surely as a suicide bomber. Human-caused but unintentional events can be threats as well — a drunk driver plowing his car into a sanctuary filled with people, or a train derailment that results in an explosion and toxic gas release[1].

Types of threats

In this book, we classify threats into two basic categories. While both pose danger of damage, destruction, loss, and death, how they present that danger — and how they're dealt with — are very different.

The first type of threat, and the one most people think about when security is discussed, is the hostile threat: the people, and their actions, that are targeted at hurting something or someone specific. The hostile threat is always caused by a human being, and is always deliberate (in the sense that harm is the goal of their actions).

The defining characteristic of hostile threats is that they are intentional; in fact, another term for them is intentional threats. The person *means* to cause harm or sow fear; that's why he's doing what he's doing.

Obvious examples of hostile threats include arsonists and active killers, but the threat can also take a less immediately sinister form — the stalker or sneak thief are good (and often overlooked) examples.

The second type is the unintentional threat. These threats are non-hostile and spring from accidents, negligence, or coincidence. They can be caused by humans or be the result of natural occurrences.

But this doesn't mean they aren't dangerous. A distracted driver isn't acting intentionally, but can be a lethal threat to everyone around him. The threat they pose is non-hostile, because there is no intent to do harm.

Other examples of unintentional threats include industrial accidents, mechanical failures, and electrical fires. Natural disasters such as hurricanes, earthquakes, and tornados are also unintentional threats. All have the potential to injure, kill, and destroy — sometimes on a massive scale.

Perspectives can be limiting

Intentional human threats are the biggest concerns of most congregations. The rise in religious extremism around the world, coupled with homegrown intolerance and the occasional mentally unbalanced spree killer, makes it easy to understand why a group of worshippers might present an attractive target. Protecting against those threats is a rational course of action.

However, it's easy to fall into the trap of thinking hostile threats are always ***external*** to the worship community. Don't let a fixation on the threats from outside the congregation limit intelligence gathering and assessment. The sad reality is that too many security plans focus on the terrorist or unknown active shooter, when in reality there are threats — deadly threats — much closer to home.

Focusing on just the crazed stranger is short-sighted. A surprising amount of the time, deadly threats come from people known to their victims, and that's something the safety planning (and any first responders) needs to reconcile if everyone is to be kept safe.

Finally, remember that unintentional threats can be just as dangerous as the intentional ones. In many cases it may actually be more important to plan for the unintentional threats. If a congregation is in that swath of the U.S. known as "tornado alley," for example, it may be more important for them to plan for sheltering people from a tornado than from foreign terrorists.

Match Targets and Threats

As you go through this process, it is critical to identify targets before making a list of possible threats. Otherwise, the result is a list of threats that have no targets!

If a target doesn't exist or isn't applicable to the congregation, there is nothing to attract a threat in the first place. There is no reason to worry about a threat that will never be there, and therefore no reason to spend the time, money, and effort it takes to prepare for that threat. Congregations without on-site schools, for instance, don't need to worry about the kinds of attacks that tend to target children.

Threat assessment and intelligence

The purpose of threat assessment is to identify the most likely dangers to the worship community. It involves gathering intelligence on (gaining knowledge of) intentional threats from human actors (participants in an action) as well as knowledge of likely natural and unintentional (accidental) human actions.

The main objective of this activity is to detect or predict danger as early as possible, so it can be met with an overwhelming response to reduce the impact on the pre-identified target. Threat assessment includes pre-identifying individuals or plausible events that are a danger, while threat intelligence involves continuously collecting and evaluating information on both existing and evolving threats.

Threat assessment and intelligence are somewhat interrelated, as assessment requires a funnel of information — raw data — that enables the identification plausible threats. Once it's been decided that a particular threat presents a plausible danger, intelligence gathering supplies the information needed to put safeguards in place. Those safeguards include mechanisms to detect attacks as early as possible in order to protect the targets.

. . .

In their best form, threat assessment and intelligence are a continuous process, because intentional human threats change over time. New actors come onto the scene, others disappear, while some evolve their targets and attack styles.

The type of threat determines the intelligence needed

Threat intelligence for incidents caused by nature or accident is a fairly stable activity. If a worship community is in a tornado zone, they should already know tornados are a threat and should automatically be added to the list that comes out of threat assessment.

The ongoing tracking of those types of events — the threat intelligence — is normally left to others, such as dedicated teams who chase storms and can deliver a tornado warning even before one hits the ground. Communities and governments have put in place electronic detection and warning systems that provide information as far ahead of time as possible, which is a good part of the reason tornado deaths have trended sharply downward in the last few decades[2].

Similarly, electronic systems can detect a fire when it is just a small smolder and alert people in the building and the fire department. Threat intelligence solutions for these and similar dangers is typically simple to find and easy to implement. Most of the work, in fact, comes down to practicing the proper responses to the alerts provided.

Intelligence gathering and assessment for intentional human threats requires more work. We can track hurricanes with a great deal of accuracy, but we can't as easily identify a potential spree killer before he strikes. How do we predict what a living being who can make decisions and change his mind will do?

. . .

The human (intentional) threat

Developing intelligence on human threats isn't easy, but it's not hopeless either. In this section, we'll consider what to look for.

Keep in mind we may not be talking about a specific person, but rather a small group of potential attackers that should be considered separately from the population around them.

Identifying intentional threats has two aspects: First, we look at the goal of the threat; what is he after? Second, what is he doing that makes us worry?

What does he want?

The goal of any threat, any attacker or thief, is to get to his target (whatever that is). In order to do this, he needs to be able to breach existing safeguards.

Yet not all humans are the same, and therefore not all attackers possess the same motivation, dedication, or skill to breach those safeguards and get to the target. From a threat intelligence perspective, we need to understand the types of attacks we may encounter in order to gather intelligence about them.

Predatory attackers, those who choose their targets for specific reasons and usually plan their attacks, typically use one or a combination of the following methods:

- Overt: The overt attacker wants to be known. He wants his targets to be aware of his approach to sow anticipation and fear. He often uses noise as part of the attack to distract the target. Political attackers are frequently of the overt variety, as they want their victims to know why they're being attacked.
- Covert: The covert attacker attempts to blend into the environment, to disguise themselves and get closer to the target without being noticed. They very often pose as members of the community to get inside any security or defenses. Most thieves, for example, are covert attackers. Covert attackers usually, but not always, expect to get away with their crimes undetected.
- Ambush: Quiet and careful in approach, violent and surprising in attack. Ambush attackers value the ability to surprise their victims and often use environmental features to hide their presence until they can spring.

If an attacker encounters resistance during their attack, they have options: fight, surrender, flee, or — especially in the case of mass killers — commit suicide. In fact, a majority of mass killers choose to end their own lives so they won't be caught. They often do so at the slightest resistance from their victims or the security team assigned to the venue.

Why does he worry us?

It's easy to figure out what might be attractive to an attacker, because doing so is an inwardly focused activity. In other words, it involves looking at the things and people in the worship community in light of how an attacker might look at them.

Watching for signs of an attack is much harder, because it requires focusing outward, perhaps even to people and groups beyond the worship community. This involves looking for patterns of activity, considering "trigger dates" (anniversaries or other events that might compel an attacker to strike), and finding ways to keep up on what's going on in the immediate world outside the congregation.

Here's an example: Many multiple victim attacks in places of worship have been domestic spillovers, meaning that they were the result of a domestic incident that happened to involve someone in the congregation. It's not unusual for a person whose relationship is ending to choose their partner's church as the place to carry out his attack. If that attack happens in the middle of services and some other people get killed as well, it serves in his mind to magnify his heartache. It delivers the messages that he's not responsible for their breakup, and his partner's worship community contributed to their problems.

This means that keeping track of people who are experiencing relationship issues is an important part of threat intelligence. It also means that if the congregation offers counseling for couples, it might at some point be the target of the person who blames that counseling for their breakup.

From a practical standpoint, this might mean training the First Responder Team members and greeters to look for signs of stress and alienation in previously happy couples. It might mean adding discreet security to counseling sessions. It might even mean holding counseling sessions off-site to reduce the tendency for transference of blame.

Look for warning signs

We know from history that many attackers follow a similar process in planning their attacks. When we say "planning," this doesn't necessarily mean the attacker has done formal analysis, drawn up blueprints, and made big whiteboards in his study with dozens of surveillance photographs. That only happens in the movies!

. . .

Planning for an intentional attack may happen only in the attacker's mind, and it may be a relatively short process. Even in seemingly random attacks, often the basic outline of the incident is decided beforehand and a target that best fits into the plan is sought out.

Also, not all attackers follow this process exactly. Some spend more time on particular steps than others, while some may skip certain steps altogether. But if intelligence gathering is tuned for looking at the tell-tale signs of the steps, there is a good chance of detecting an attack before it can occur.

At the very least, it may enable the alerting of first responders so they are prepared ahead of the potential threat.

Let's walk through the steps an attacker might use in planning and executing an attack:

- *Preliminary Target Selection:* An attacker decides upon a target he'd would like to attack. This may be a specific target, or simply a decision about the general parameters of the target.
- *Initial Surveillance:* The attacker begins a hasty evaluation of the target to determine if he feels an attack would be successful. This may happen relatively quickly and can be very difficult to spot.
- *Final Target Selection:* Sometimes, once a specific target has been selected, the attacker obsesses over it. If this happens, he'll move into the next step of surveillance.
- *Pre-Attack Surveillance:* The obsessive attacker may try to learn as much about the target as possible. He may do internet research, repeatedly visiting the congregation's website or social media pages. In this age of ever-cheaper technology, he

may use things such as drones to gather his images, videos, and possibly even audio.

- *Planning:* The attacker takes the raw data collected and begins to put together a plan. Again, the plan will probably not be written on paper, but formulated in the attacker's mind.
- *Rehearsal:* One thing we've noticed is that an intentional attacker almost always does a rehearsal of his attack. It might be done mere minutes before the attack, sometimes within hours, but other times it may be weeks in advance. Many times it's done while trying to blend in with others.
- *Execution:* The actual attack sequence, where the damage is done. At this point the only option is response by the people charged with security.
- *Escape* (or suicide): The attacker may or may not have an escape plan. If an attack is successful, most have some plan of how to get away from the incident scene. It may be as simple as running down the sidewalk, or as complex as having a stolen car available. If the attack is unsuccessful or interrupted in some way, the attacker often kills himself rather than be taken into custody.

Warning signs

In its most effective form, threat analysis is based on actions and behaviors — what people *do* rather than who they are.

Many people fixate on "profiling" or building a picture of a potential attacker, then looking for people who fit that profile. This really isn't possible for institutions that don't have a large staff and police powers, and even then has dubious value.

For the rest of us, it's more productive (and easier) to look for the signs displayed by someone who is planning or may decide to plan an attack. That type of information is likely to be useful in identifying a pending attack.

. . .

Because of the nature of this kind of intelligence gathering, it's not something that can be easily accomplished outside of the worship community. While it's possible to spot the signs of an immediately pending attack, it's impossible to spot earlier signs in the population-at-large. The further outside the congregation, the harder it is to see warning signs.

But as we've noted, many attackers come from inside the community. This is where a significant portion of intelligence gathering should be directed.

Red flags

The basic concept is to look for telltale signs — "red flags" — that may indicate a potential or impending attack. These are actions or signals people give off either as part of their personality or as a natural byproduct of pre-attack activities.

One red flag might be the appearance of a stranger at services, in a congregation where newcomers are not common. Another red flag might be a car parked for an inordinate amount of time across the street, or one left in the parking lot after services (or there before services).

A common red flag is the person who holds a grievance against the congregation in general — or some specific members, such as clergy or lay counselors. Strangers driving past the facilities during services, or lingering in an obvious attempt to observe the comings and goings, are all red flags pointing to initial surveillance.

. . .

Someone approaching congregation members and asking questions, or using a cellphone to take photos/videos at specific times are signs of a possible attack in the planning stages. Website visits from the same IP (internet address) or multiple calls from the same telephone number (especially if they happen during non-business hours) may be other signs.

Clustering

Of course none of those red flags is, in itself, proof of an impending attack. A stranger taking pictures of the facilities may be nothing more than someone intrigued with the architecture or history of the building. Questions from a stranger may be a newcomer looking for a place to bring his family.

One behavior, taken by itself, is likely not indicative of anything. Two such behaviors might be slightly more concerning, but each additional behavior adds exponentially to the threat assessment. This is called "clustering": the appearance of several signs in a short time period, or in the same area, or with the same person.

Any of those things mentioned (and many more) aren't necessarily of concern individually, but when added to the cluster may signal a potential problem.

Look for warning signs of domestic issues, public threats, property vandalism, and other out-of-the-norm behaviors.

Gathering intelligence and preventing trouble

Gathering the threat intelligence needed to identify possible avenues of attack can be done in a number of ways. Sometimes simply starting the intelligence gathering process causes a threat to seek an easier target.

The intelligence funnel

We refer to the collection and processing of these bits of information and signs as an intelligence funnel. Lots of data comes in at the top, and it's directed to the people who can best evaluate it and do something with it.

The First Responder Team, for instance, will probably see a lot of things in the course of their duties that merit closer inspection. They're the mouth of the funnel, and in a properly designed security system will funnel that information to the Safety Council at large, who can sort and evaluate it.

Similarly, the non-involved members of the congregation who find something concerning should be encouraged to pass that information, in confidence, to someone on the Safety Council. Encourage them to do so in a timely manner, so the information can be evaluated and actions taken if deemed necessary.

Clergy, councilors, and religious studies teachers should also have a way of reporting information to be evaluated. Establish a clear method by which those concerned can report information, along with a protocol for how it should be handled and by whom.

Get closer to the congregational family

In this day of accessible social media and related technology, it's easy to look at a screen and think we know someone. Beyond the selfies and cat memes, though, there's a real person with real things going on in their lives.

As people who are part of the same religious group, the members of the congregation probably have similar interests and goals in life. Religion is a big part of their lives, and one reason to be a member of a worship community is to be part of a group that helps each other attain those goals. Yet, far too often we have no clue that someone's son is having a rough time making friends at school or someone's ex-husband has been threatening her.

Getting close to the congregational family is a vital part of a security plan. Let's take Jill, for example. She's really good at hiding what's going on in her personal life. She shows up regularly to worship, helps teach a Sunday school class, and always has a smile on her face. Others in the congregation have been friends with her on social media for years. Not once has she ever said anything about her ex-husband.

If people were to really get to know Jill as a person, though, they might find out that her ex-husband has been threatening her. They would then also know he's a potential threat to the rest of the community whenever she's there. It's not her fault, but the rest of the congregation may be at risk.

Were the people in charge of security planning aware of the situation, they could use that information to discreetly alert the security staff to be aware of what he looks like and what vehicle he drives. Does he own any weapons? Does he have a criminal record? Does she have a restraining order on him? These are all important things to know to properly gauge the threat level. Knowing this would both protect Jill and everyone around her.

· · ·

Part of the threat intelligence function, then, is getting to know — really know — the people who are all gathered in the same building anywhere from one to several hours a week.

Furthermore, get to know the visitors too. This won't be a hard sell. We can't imagine any clergy or lay leadership having a problem with you getting to know the people you go to worship with better, and that includes those who are new to the congregation.

A word of caution on this topic: Ensure that the information gathered, particularly that which is told in confidence, stays limited to the Safety Council and shared only on a need-to-know basis. This is privileged information and should be used solely for the purposes of detecting, identifying, and preventing an attack. This is a very valuable tool if used correctly, and the last thing anyone wants is to be accused of gossiping.

Don't ignore the signs

It's easy to be dismissive of threat indicators. They come from multiple places, sometimes come in large quantities, and often seem to be unrelated to anything in particular. Sifting through this information is a chore. When looking at things that ultimately prove to be irrelevant, it can be easy to miss something that is relevant.

We admit this is easier said than done, particularly in light of what we said about the value of any given sign. But having a process in place to properly deal with the influx of intelligence makes this easier — and makes clustering easier to spot.

Have a system in place to collect the information that comes from others, and pass it along to those who can evaluate its worth. With several people looking at any piece of information, it's much easier to determine whether that piece of data does or does not reveal a risk and whether it needs to be addressed.

Clustering is applicable to this evaluation as well. If several people are looking at the same information, and only one thinks it's an issue, it might not be. If several conclude that it is, it's probably a sign it should be taken seriously.

Take warnings seriously

In many active-shooter and terrorist incidents, the lack of action by decision makers is justified after the fact with the excuse that "there were no specific credible threats."

What exactly were they expecting? That the killer would call them up ahead of time and say, "I'm going to be shooting up your church on Sunday between the hours of 9:50 and 10am. I'll be driving a white four-door sedan. See you then"?

Even then we wonder how specific something has to be to be "credible." What if he didn't specify their address, or perhaps didn't specify exactly which Sunday?

We see this over and over as we study attacks and attackers. Early warning signs are often dismissed because no one wants to look like they are over-reacting. No one wants to be "that guy" who caused people to panic when nothing eventually happened. No one wants to look foolish.

At the same time, early warning indicators need to be taken seriously.

Some kinds of red flags are more urgent and carry more weight than others; when clustered, the concern should go up dramatically.

Threat intelligence is a powerful tool *if* it's listened to. Yes, there may be times when the tornado sirens go off and no tornado materializes. But it's our considered opinion that it would be better to explain why preparations were made for something that didn't happen than explain why no preparations were made for something that did happen — especially when there were clues beforehand.

Put intelligence gathering systems in place and trust the output. If it's wrong and nothing happens, count it as a good training exercise and get ready for the next one.

Specific types of attacks

Up to now, we've looked at threat intelligence from the types of incidents, warning signs, and sources of information, and stressed the importance of not ignoring or dismissing warning signs. Now let's look at some specific types of threats and indicators of an attack.

While not necessarily exclusive to religious institutions, in some cases certain attacks tend to be concentrated on faith communities. They also tend to have specific, identifiable markers or red flags that may serve as advance warning.

The active killer

The active killer is the person who attacks a large group with intent to cause mass casualties. This is sometimes referred to as an "active shooter," though that term is a misnomer (perhaps the result of a political point of view), because mass-casualty attacks have been committed with guns, knives, bombs, gasoline, and even vehicles.

Why is this detail important? As intelligence is being gathered, it's important to consider that a potential attacker who is obsessed with fire is just as much of a risk to life as the person who has interest in and access to firearms. Don't allow a fixation on one type of attacker to blind the process to the unnoticed one who's already present but doesn't fit the preconceptions.

An active killer incident has three defining characteristics. First is the continuous infliction of casualties until intervention, in the form of resisting victims or law enforcement, causes the attacker to stop. The active killer doesn't have a fixed or specific number of victims in mind. The killing continues until the attacker is stopped or runs out of immediate victims.

The second characteristic is that the active killer attack often has a component of domestic violence. Spouses, children, or even parents are often killed before the attacker kills others. These associated deaths may be in a separate location, or may be in the same location and at the same time as the rest of the victims.

Finally, the active killer very often commits suicide when confronted by law enforcement, resisting victims, or even uninvolved bystanders. Many mass-casualty attacks are murder/suicides, planned in advance. The murders are sometimes a byproduct of the suicide, a way of punctuating the killer's exit from this earth and attempting to place blame for his actions on others.

.   .   .

Because active killers tend to have some commonality in their planning patterns, they usually give off warning signs of an impending attack.

Before selecting a target, they'll often tell someone about their desire to kill themselves and/or other people. They may write articles, poems, or even songs about violent deaths. They may make violent drawings or sketches. They may use a remark about mass violence as a veiled threat during a verbal confrontation. These are all indicators that need to be reported — and taken seriously by those to whom they are reported.

As they go through their planning process, they will do surveillance and, in many cases, even a "dry run" or practice attack. If someone is spotted in the parking lot, just sitting in his car (especially at odd hours), that may be a sign of surveillance or a dry run. Because of normalcy bias, such clues tend to be dismissed or explained away.

There is an important point that needs to be understood about the active killer attack on a house of worship: It's rarely going to be a complete stranger. In most of the cases we've studied, the attacker had been to the place of worship before. Some were themselves regulars, or the spouse of a frequent attendee.

As part of an exercise, we often have our students answer this: "Assume you've been told your congregation will be attacked in 30 days, and that the attacker is someone you've seen before. Who do you think it is?"

It's surprising how often a name comes immediately to mind, because the subconscious is very good about evaluating information without the bias and preconception of the conscious mind. Do this exercise as part of the planning process; if a name comes to someone's mind quickly, and particularly if more than one person comes up with the same name, it's important to investigate and figure out why. We'd also recommend that safeguards be in place immediately.

This is a useful exercise for the greeters to do, especially if the greeters are members of a First Responder Team. Even if a name doesn't present itself immediately, have them think about this exercise as they greet people entering the place of worship. Most communities gather information on visitors so they can better contact them in the future. How about collecting information, including others' impressions, to gauge if the person is a potential threat?

As people of faith, it is easy to want to give others the benefit of the doubt. This often causes us to dismiss what might be an obvious indicator. Resist that temptation and consciously focus on the responsibilities of safety and security planning.

The religious terrorist

The term terrorist has been used so often it has lost its original meaning. Many today would consider an active killer a terrorist, and while there is no doubt he causes terror in his victims, his behavior and motivations are not that of a terrorist in the truest sense of the term. Although they might have many similarities, the active killer and the religious terrorist have different motivations.

The active killer is motivated by a personal affront or perceived social injustice, or sometimes a deteriorating relationship that he blames on others. The religious terrorist, on the other hand, is motivated by religious radicalization to strike for the glory of the deity as worshipped by his sect. He believes he is doing holy work by clearing the unbelievers away and laying the groundwork for the conversion of the populace.

Examples? On November 2, 2010, a group affiliated with al-Qaeda and known as the Islamic State of Iraq and the Levant (ISIL), or the Islamic State of Iraq and al-Sham (ISIS), issued a threat: "All Christian centers, organizations and institutions, leaders and followers are legitimate targets for the *mujahideen* (Muslim fighters) wherever they can reach them[3]."

This was followed by several church bombings across the Middle East over the 2010 Christmas and 2011 New Year's holidays. Radical Islamic supporters including the late Adam Gadahn, an American-born terrorist, have specifically encouraged the targeting and kidnapping of Western Christian missionary workers[4].

While we think of terrorists as being foreigners, we also have our own homegrown domestic religious terrorists who may be inspired by their brethren in distant lands. The list of American terrorist groups and individuals seems to grow after each attack, as we learn their affiliations, intentions, and methods.

With religious terrorists, the goal is often to kill or capture and convert. They are often funded from out of the country but must collect all their resources locally. The act of gathering and assembling resources leaves telltale traces, but very few of those indicators will be visible to an internal intelligence funnel. To get this kind of information, seek outside connections in law enforcement and Homeland Security.

Threat intelligence on terrorists

It's important for threat intelligence operations to stay in touch with larger sources of information on potential terrorists. Start with local law enforcement. Most agencies have gang task forces that often also track local terrorism suspects, and the bigger police departments may even have officers specifically assigned to tracking suspected terrorists.

The local FBI office will have information on identified and suspected threats that they'll share with bonafide representatives of potential target groups, and the Department of Homeland Security maintains regional Intelligence Fusion Centers, which "operate as state and major urban area focal points for the receipt, analysis, gathering, and sharing of threat-related information between federal; state, local, tribal, territorial (SLTT); and private sector partners[5]."

Both of the authors have spent many hours in meetings with these local, regional, and national law enforcement agencies in order to develop a picture of what might threaten the institutions we were charged with protecting. Any organized Safety Council should do the same.

This isn't to say that broad intelligence can't be developed internally. Stay abreast of what's happening overseas, paying particular attention to the kind of attacks being perpetrated. Tactics used overseas often make their way to our country. For example, vehicular attacks first showed up in the Middle East, then spread to Europe, and are now being seen in our country.

When an attack in a foreign land makes the news, look at both the target and the methodology. Who or what groups were targeted? Why were they chosen? Look at how the attack happened, and ask if the safeguards in place are sufficient to thwart a similar attack?

· · ·

There is some good news in this: Many of the same safeguards that protect from an active killer will also help with the religious terrorist. Their planning, rehearsal, and execution stages are very much alike, since their end goal — many deaths — is the same. While their motivations may differ, they share many of the same planning traits.

Coordinated symphonic attacks

A coordinated symphonic attack is a multi-step or multi-actor attack whose scope or complexity requires more than a single person, weapon, or location for effectiveness.

In a multi-step incident, the attacks generally come in waves. The initial attack will occur, then a secondary (and even subsequent) attack is launched a short period of time later. Because there are brief periods between the waves people tend to think the attack is over, which exposes them to the secondary attack.

For example, a trend in bombing attacks is to place a secondary device that explodes several minutes after the initial blast. The goal of the second device (the second wave) is to injure or kill first responders, fleeing victims, and good samaritans.

A successful multi-step attack usually requires more than one person to initiate successfully. Many active killer and terrorist attacks are symphonic attacks, involving two or more criminal actors working in tandem to initiate the overall attack.

A good example of a symphonic attack is the Columbine High School massacre of 1999. The two attackers were close friends and planned the attack together over a long period of time. Working together, they placed two backpacks containing propane tank bombs in the school cafeteria prior to the attack.

The plan was to detonate the bombs at lunchtime, in the hope of killing hundreds of students who would be gathered in the cafeteria. The second part of the plan was to shoot the surviving students as they fled the cafeteria. Thankfully, the bombs were not built well and did not detonate as intended, limiting the number of casualties. As bad as it was, it was intended to be much worse.

After the Columbine attack, many other attacks included the coordinated placement of pipe bombs or other improvised explosive devices (IEDs) in addition to shooting.

Other multi-step symphonic attacks have involved shooting and Molotov cocktails, or simply gasoline and a match. In the attacks on a U.S. diplomatic compound in Benghazi, Libya in 2012, gasoline was used to force the locked-down ambassador and security team to leave the safety of the bunker and into a position where they could be killed.

Because of its multiple attack vectors, a coordinated symphonic attack is difficult to stop once initiated. Detecting them as early as possible is the key to stopping these attacks, or at least reducing the victim count.

As with other types of attacks, there is an identifiable planning cycle similar to what has already been discussed. The big difference is that because there are multiple attackers, they have more people to do the necessary pre-attack surveillance. Being able to detect surveillance activity and the staging of the actual attack is key.

.   .   .

Because of their similarities, always assume that every mass-casualty incident is a coordinated attack — until the circumstances prove otherwise. Are there suspicious vehicles or people staged outside of the initial attack area? Are potential attackers moving to a secondary location?

Evacuation or shelter plans, for instance, need to take into account the possibility of a coordinated attack. Having people exit the building and gather in the parking lot is a common plan that is easily guessed by any savvy attacker. Putting a couple of car bombs in the parking lot set to detonate a few minutes after the main attack would be an excellent way to inflict secondary casualties.

These sound like common-sense things that would be easily noticed. Yes, they are — but only if someone is actively looking for them. The reality is, most people are not looking for these things, so they don't take note of them or dismiss them as insignificant. The planning and rehearsal for a symphonic attack may not be noticed until its last phases. This is why it's important to be looking for the telltale signs and, more importantly, have a structure in place that guarantees someone is looking and doing something with the information being gathered.

Arson

Arson at places of worship goes way back in American history. It has been a favorite attack for generations, and many such incidents have targeted our minority religious institutions such as African-American churches and Jewish synagogues.

Records of religious arson attacks go back to at least the 1820s. During the fight for civil rights in the 1960s, arson on predominantly black churches (and the synagogues of their Jewish supporters) became a frequent method of intimidation. Those attacks continued into the 1980s, prompting Congress to pass the Church Arson Prevention Act in 1996. As part of that legislation, the National Church Arson Task Force was authorized by President Bill Clinton.

The aim of the legislation and task force was to combat then-increasing arson at all houses of worship. Although the number of such attacks has dropped in recent years, arson is still a high risk for most places of worship. It's an easy method of intimidation and revenge that involves little planning, raises few red flags, and requires almost no skill.

Although the motives of an arsonist are important, it's enough to understand that arson attacks still follow the same patterns of planning as the other types of attacks we've discussed. Target selection, surveillance, and planning patterns are similar to other attacks, and the same safeguards used to mitigate them also have a great deal of overlap for arson attacks.

The one major difference is that the arsonist rarely wants to die for his cause. Arsonists plan to escape, and in particular to escape unnoticed. This is understandable when the aspect of intimidation is factored in. The unseen attacker is more frightening than the person standing in handcuffs. The arsonist's goal is to get away "clean."

Because of this, arson frequently occurs when no one is in the building. Detecting arson using threat intelligence is a combination of watching for surveillance patterns (particularly after hours), looking for signs of antagonism or disaffection within the community, and having proper fire-detection systems in place.

. . .

Arsonists frequently develop a fascination with fire as children. They are overwhelmingly white males between 17 and 26 years of age[6], although female arsonists are not unknown. Many arsonists were subjected to some sort of social isolation when young, which generally leads to conduct disorders. Cruelty to animals and property destruction are prime indicators of a potential arsonist.

As in so many other instances, having a good connection with the members of the worship community facilitates the detection of telltale behavior patterns. Being aware of those signs may allow detection of arson attacks that might originate from within the membership. More importantly, being aware of those who have this potential can provide the opportunity to get them the help they need. Preventing someone from developing into an arsonist is both a noble act and a way to protect the community.

Mental health issues

Dealing with people who have mental health issues can be extremely challenging and can easily exceed the average person's ability. Put those people into an open, trusting place of worship and they can destroy lives.

An unfortunate few know the damage a person with untreated mental health issues can cause. For those who have lived through that trauma, it is an experience they try to forget.

While this may be hard to accept, places of worship are often a refuge for people with severe mental health issues. In many congregations, the clergy function as front-line therapists, and some worship communities actually have ministries that focus on therapy for mental health issues. These activities enable them to address both the spiritual and mental health issues the person might be dealing with.

· · ·

The more organized the outreach, the more likely the congregation is to have properly licensed therapists with the training to diagnose mental health issues. In the best cases, they work with psychiatrists who can prescribe medication and admit patients to facilities that provide round-the-clock crisis care.

But most congregations are not so organized. Their clergy may not have the extensive training or contacts needed to handle mental health cases and thus have limited treatment options. They typically provide only spiritual advice and very basic therapy sessions.

Those conducting such sessions may not have the knowledge or experience required to deal with people who need serious psychiatric care. They may be a comfort to people with mild cases of depression, but it's easy for them to get in over their heads when dealing with someone who has severe mental health issues.

The difficulty is that some patients actually seek out organizations with limited care options to avoid being medicated or hospitalized. What's worse, many religion-based therapists are unwilling to turn over a patient to a psychiatrist because they fear losing the religious connection with the patient. The desire to help someone spiritually sometimes blinds them to the severity of the patient's illness.

Occasionally, they are fooled into thinking the issues are common behavioral problems that can be solved just by praying with the patient. They may not discover how severe the mental health issues are until it's too late. This leaves places of worship extremely vulnerable to people with specific types of mental health issues.

· · ·

A good example are people with severe Narcissistic Personality Disorder (NPD). Take a group of trusting, well-intentioned people who sincerely strive to help others and add in a religious obligation to do so, and there exists an environment that is extremely attractive to a narcissistic predator. Those qualities of compassion and trust that most consider strengths, the person with narcissistic mental health issues sees as a weakness that can be exploited.

It's easy to believe that someone with severe mental issues is easily spotted, but that's not always the case. Psychologist Stephen Johnson writes[7] that a narcissist is someone who has "buried his true self-expression in response to early injuries and replaced it with a highly developed, compensatory false self." In other words, they wear masks — and they're experts at it. They're accomplished at hiding their true selves and their motives until it's too late.

Covert narcissists are dangerous. Their tactics convince others they are perfectly normal. They are master manipulators and quite possibly the most dangerous predators on the planet. They are also attracted to religious groups, where they can operate freely in a trusting environment.

Since people with NPD often target places of worship, it's sensible for people in positions of authority to know what they are up against and how to safeguard against them.

The covert narcissist often plays the victim and attempts to conceal who they are behind their chosen mask. The covert narcissist is especially dangerous when they're female; it's much easier for a female narcissist to get sympathy and use that to control others to get what she wants. The authors have seen these people completely destroy a place of worship from the inside.

. . .

Although it's beyond the scope of this book to get into all the tactics of a narcissist, it is critical that any risk management plan includes training and appropriate response to the manipulations of a person with NPD.

Places of worship and people who attend them are at great risk from those who are suffering from severe mental health ailments. They are at risk not just physically, but also emotionally. The reputation of the institution may even be at stake. People with mental health issues pose a great risk of harm to leaders, members, and even themselves.

As risk managers, we must take time to learn about mental health issues (including, but not limited to, narcissism) and be on the lookout for "wolves in sheep's clothing." When they're encountered, they must be quickly addressed before they can destroy lives.

Places of worship need to accept their limitations and get people in crisis the help they need.

Sexual assault

One of the most difficult parts of writing a book is addressing issues that have impacted the lives of people close to you. With statistics showing that every 98 seconds, someone is sexually assaulted in this country[8], it's not a stretch to say we likely all know someone who has been impacted by sexual assault.

We have to accept the possibility that someone with whom we worship has been, or currently is, the victim of sexual assault. We must sadly also accept the reality that some of those attacks may occur in connection with our worship community.

There are numerous documented cases of sexual assault among youth group leaders, clergy, religious school teachers, volunteers — the list goes on. One study conducted by Gene Abel, M.D., and Nora Harlow concluded that 93% of those who had admitted to sexual assault of children also considered themselves religious people[9]. Combine that with the fact that the majority of sexual assaults are committed by someone the victim knows, and it's not hard to see a potential vulnerability in our places of worship.

The simple reality is that our places of worship are a prime hunting ground for sexual predators. We have youth groups, religious school classes, and all kinds of extracurricular activities where predators can access victims. The chance for an assault under such conditions is very high.

To make things worse, religious institutions are traditionally very bad at handling these crimes. Far too many places of worship want to keep these incidents "under wraps" — to handle them internally and not involve law enforcement. The standard operating procedure is to convince the victim not to report the crime, and pray for (and with) the sexual predator.

We want to state this categorically: This approach is immoral, unethical, and most likely criminal. At least 98% of rapists never spend a day in jail[10]; many of the attacks are never reported. Religious institutions need to stop being part of the problem and start being part of the solution. To use a Christian metaphor, we should be flipping the tables of the temple over if we even get a hint of this happening.

· · ·

Furthermore, there should be no place on this planet more suited to helping a person recover from a sexual assault than our places of worship. We should be prepared to get the right people, including law enforcement, involved to help the victims. Despite the differences in the authors' backgrounds, we are in complete agreement that dismissing these events out of kindness for the attacker is one of the vilest acts people of faith can commit.

We believe it our moral responsibility to contact law enforcement when a crime has been committed, and sexual assault is a crime. To even put together an internal investigation before contacting law enforcement will be justifiably looked at as a coverup. Our advice is simple: Don't mess around with this. ***Call the police.***

From a threat detection perspective, we need to know what sexual predators look like and how they operate. Although we want to catch these incidents before they occur, we also need to be looking for attacks that might have already occurred (or are occurring). This means we need to be alert to the signs of sexual abuse.

Sexual predators have some common characteristics. Predators tend to attack in environments where the likelihood of getting caught is low, so they do things that let them get close to potential victims, and have personality traits that allow them to dominate.

Like red flags for attackers, one of these by itself is probably not a cause for concern. But when clusters of these characteristics appear in the same person, that may be a sign something more sinister is afoot[11]:

- Often married or in long-term relationships
- Sexualizes or objectifies women
- Displays arrogance (often excused as confidence)

- Constantly tries to convince people they are trustworthy
- Needs to be powerful and in control
- Tends toward rationalization and justification
- Blames others or circumstances for their failures
- Displays a sense of entitlement
- Is an insistent helper/volunteer, won't take no for an answer
- Inserts themselves into stressful and vulnerable situations of potential victims
- Portrays false empathy
- Attracted to both males and females and may attack both

This is by no means an exhaustive list of warning signs. Seek out guidance from professional organizations that deal with sexual assaults and predation, like the Rape, Abuse & Incest National Network (RAINN). Encourage the First Responder Team(s), as well as the entire congregation, to take their training and learn how to look for warning signs.

Any place of worship can be part of the solution by playing an important role in stopping sexual violence and connecting survivors with the support they deserve. If anyone in the congregation suspects or has been made aware of a sexual assault, they should be encouraged to contact law enforcement immediately. If the victim refuses to talk to law enforcement, help them contact the National Sexual Assault Hotline at 1-800-656-HOPE or online at www.rainn.org.

A special note about suicide

Many people with severe mental health issues, or those who have been victims of emotionally charged crimes such as sexual assault, are at risk for self-harm.

It's important to understand that a person threatening suicide or displaying any traits of self-harm is in crisis and needs immediate emergency care. Failing to contact professionals who are capable of helping the person is not only irresponsible, it's immoral and unethical.

Anyone with knowledge of someone threatening suicide or self-harm should contact the National Suicide Prevention Lifeline at 1-800-273-8255 immediately! If the person is in immediate danger or is unwilling to get help, call 911 (or the local emergency number in your country). Make sure that dispatch understands that the person is threatening suicide or self-harm.

VULNERABILITY & RISK ASSESSMENT

Targets are things (and people) that might be chosen (by a human threat) or be in the path (nature/accident) of danger. Threats are active dangers that pose a risk of loss to the targets.

Vulnerabilities are where the targets and threats meet; they're those aspects of the target that are at risk from the threat. Vulnerabilities are the people or things that are susceptible to being wounded, damaged, or destroyed; things that are open to assault; things that are difficult to defend. A target might be a building; a threat might be a hurricane; the vulnerabilities are those parts of the building that might sustain damage should the hurricane hit.

Once a target has been identified and what threats it faces ascertained, figuring out where the vulnerabilities are will indicate what to protect and where, how, and when to protect it.

Imagine trying to identify vulnerabilities without first identifying targets and threats — it would be a daunting, perhaps impossible task! The concept of Target-Based Risk Management, that of calm and reasoned analysis, dramatically reduces the work needed in vulnerability assessment.

Don't neglect to do the work in the previous Target and Threat Assessment chapters. It's tempting to skip that dry stuff but, without narrowing things down, listing the vulnerabilities can quickly become overwhelming. That's because there are a lot of things that are vulnerable, but not all of them are within the scope of a protection plan. Even if they are, it may not be possible to protect them given the resources available.

Start with the environment

Targets inherit the vulnerabilities of the environments in which they exist, so we must begin by finding the vulnerabilities of those environments and then move to the targets themselves. Environments can refer to locations, movements, groups, or time. Each change presents a new environment that might have dramatically different vulnerabilities.

If, for example, the clergy has been determined to be at risk, and they live somewhere other than the campus (or travel to visit the sick in the community), that presents a mobile vulnerability: multiple locations, travel through perhaps multiple neighborhoods, and at various times. This requires a vulnerability profile for the target in each environment through which they travel or in which they spend time. Targets that are mobile (i.e., not tied to one place and one time) are particularly difficult to protect and can easily use up significant protective resources.

Even a stationary target may have multiple vulnerabilities because of the environments of time and group make-up. If gatherings are held on more than one day, at more than one time during the day, in more than one building on campus, or involve more than one identifiable group, those combinations present multiple vulnerabilities.

Make a map

The easiest way to track vulnerability assessment is to make a relational map. This sounds involved, but it's really nothing more than a spreadsheet with the targets listed in the left-most column and the environments listed across the top row. Make an "x" in each cell where an environment and a target meet.

For each box with an X, ask a question: "What makes this specific target, in this specific environment, susceptible to being wounded or damaged by the threats that have already been identified?" Be sure to write the answer(s) down!

What's gained from asking that question is tangible data that shows where to look for vulnerabilities. Not everything that is susceptible is necessarily a vulnerability; to determine that, a little investigation is needed.

This is a critically important step in the assessment process. The data collected here will be used in many other places. In identifying specific risk scenarios or incidents, creating the risk ratings and ranking the need for protection, and beginning the process of mitigating the risks, this information will be the guide. Resist the urge to take shortcuts!

How to find the vulnerabilities

The map made in the last step shows *where* to look — now it's necessary to learn how to look and what to look for.

How are vulnerabilities found? How does one know if they're looking the right ones? Have any been missed? Perhaps most importantly, when is it time to stop looking?

Choose the methodology

As it happens, several effective approaches to finding vulnerabilities exist. The method(s) used and how much time is spent on them will vary depending on the available resources.

The easiest method is to put the Planning Group together with the relational map of vulnerabilities, and have each person identify the vulnerabilities he/she sees for each target in each environment. This gets a lot of information out quickly, but there is a risk: the results are limited to the knowledge and experience of the participants. The more forceful group member(s) can disproportionally drive the opinions of the other participants, leading to a kind of "group think" that results in a skewed plan.

If the members of the group aren't versed in attacks of all kinds, and if they're not used to studying and understanding how attacks happen, the information developed will leave large gaps in protection. When dealing with a building's structural resistance against various kinds of non-intentional attacks, for instance, without knowing engineering or construction, it's difficult to come to informed opinions about whether a vulnerability really exists.

It's possible to work around this lack of knowledge if members of the

Safety Council are willing to educate themselves in the specialized knowledge needed in some areas.

Making use of expertise

Barring that, there is a second option in dealing with this lack of expertise: Call in an expert, or perhaps an expert team, to do this assessment for the congregation. If the Safety Council has done a thorough job in target and threat assessment, the hired experts will be able to quickly identify where vulnerabilities exist.

In this process, the experts will commonly do things like "penetration tests," where they make dry runs or simulated attacks to gauge weakness and vulnerability. Penetration tests might involve testing barriers and alarms, data security, or access control during services and events. The goals are to probe the defenses and point out the weaknesses they find.

A professional assessment is usually thorough, specific, and factual. The biggest issue with this approach is the cost. Experts in this field don't come cheap, particularly when the vulnerability assessment involves a number of targets, threats, and environments. A professional assessment takes a great deal of time, which always increases the cost.

This approach is generally used by governmental and large institutions that have the resources to throw at the problem. They can afford to buy the expertise they need. Most congregations can't.

But it's possible to combine the two approaches: Hire an expert to participate in the brainstorming and preliminary planning sessions, and use their experience and knowledge to guide the Safety Council. This gives an informed opinion and helps the group see things they might otherwise miss.

The expert may also help with specific agenda items, such as selecting security systems or hiring executive protection personnel for high-risk clergy.

This isn't to say an expert or experts are an absolutely need, of course. Many congregations are able to complete their risk management plan and implement it without outside expertise. Generally, the larger and more complex the protection task, the more it benefits from professional guidance.

Looking at history for clues

Vulnerabilities may also be gauged by using historical data. This is particularly valid for non-intentional threats. Hazard information is available from the Federal Emergency Management Agency (FEMA) and the Department of Homeland Security (DHS), as well as from state emergency management agencies. The American Red Cross (ARC) is another great resource that can help identify vulnerabilities to natural as well as manmade disasters.

While time-consuming, a large amount of information can be gleaned from interviewing people who have knowledge of past events in the community. There may even be useful historical information in the congregation's archives.

Local law enforcement can often supply information on calls they've made in and around the neighborhood, as well as the nature of those calls. These are good methods for finding vulnerabilities that are sometimes hidden — or not discussed.

. . .

Another useful way to determine vulnerabilities in a place of worship is to compare the facilities and procedures to an existing framework for auditing security controls. An excellent one is the FEMA publication #426, *"Reference Manual to Mitigate Potential Terrorist Attacks Against Buildings*[1]*"*. This is a very thorough checklist that makes it easy to spot vulnerabilities in physical facilities.

Regardless of the method(s) used, the end result should be a list of vulnerabilities that would enable a threat to harm or damage the target as it resides in each environment. Once the vulnerabilities are identified, it's easy to connect them to the kinds of incidents (scenarios) that could result in harm to the target, be it buildings or people.

That connection among those things — targets, threats, and vulnerabilities —enables the safety and security initiative to focus on what's likely, rather than becoming obsessed with fantasy scenarios. It helps to properly allocate resources (time, money, labor) to what's most important. Without it, resources can easily be wasted preparing for events that simply aren't plausible.

What incidents are likely?

Once the information about the congregation's vulnerabilities is collected, it can be turned into meaningful and actionable data. The key to doing so is identifying the kinds of incidents the threats could use to exploit those vulnerabilities.

This is where the target/environment relational map we talked about earlier comes into use. By connecting the threat information and vulnerability data that's been generated, it's easy to see what kinds of incidents are possible. Once those are listed, a picture emerges of what kind(s) of protection the congregation needs.

This process is best done (particularly if there is a whiteboard available) as a group exercise with members of the Safety Council. Being able to visualize how the items connect helps the group see relationships among targets, threats, and vulnerabilities.

The goal of this exercise is to come away with a list of incidents that, if they were to occur in the place of worship, could cause harm or damage to the identified targets. These incidents will be the basis for helping to mitigate them through plans, procedures, and training.

Examples of incidents

Let's look at an example list of some common (but generalized) incidents that come from work and consulting sessions we've conducted over the years. These are really a composite of situations we've seen, but an actual working list needs to be much more specific to the individual worship community.

To do so, start with generalized items like these. Then for each one add a few sentences describing that incident in detail. Include the target, its environment, and the threat involved. This gives the specificity you need to calculate the risks involved.

Don't try to prioritize the incidents yet; that's done in the next step, the risk calculation exercise. Right now, it's enough just to make a list. After the risk calculations have been done, the exercise can be done a second time to see if any likely incidents were missed. (This second pass often shows that there are combinations of events that could occur together, possibly where both are of lower impact or likelihood, but together they become more likely or more dangerous.)

The specificity of this information is particularly important when putting together role-player-based training scenarios.

For clarity's sake we classify these possible incidents into destructive and disruptive categories. Destructive incidents, as the name implies, cause injury, death, property damage, financial loss, or present a great possibility of causing any of those should they not be addressed properly. Destructive incidents can be natural or caused by man; they can be intentional or non-intentional.

Destructive incidents might include:

- Violent domestic issue
- Letter or mail bombs
- Natural disasters
- Hostage incidents
- Assault of clergy
- Arson
- Identity theft
- Suicide bombing
- Car bombing
- Metal theft
- Robbery
- Burglary
- Automobile theft
- Assault of members
- Kidnapping
- Vandalism

Disruptive incidents cause an interruption in the life of the worship community, but don't carry with them the high likelihood of loss or damage. Disruptive incidents are usually man-caused and often intended to annoy or intimidate members of the congregation, clergy, or staff. They often have a political or social basis.

Some examples of disruptive incidents:

- Interruption of worship
- Building intrusions
- Bomb threat
- Verbal abuse
- Incidents at clergy's residence
- Incidents at religious schools/studies
- Protests (organized or spontaneous)
- Picketing

Again, these are just examples. Each individual worship community will have different or additional concerns, and those need to be identified and described in detail.

Calculating risk

Risk is the combination of target, threat, and vulnerability, expressed in a way that gives some idea of what's most dangerous. It allows us to prioritize preparations and allocate protective resources. In other words, it tells us what's most important to deal with. Risk, therefore, is the measure by which we gauge urgency.

Risk is a combination of incidence (likelihood, or how often something happens) and consequence (impact, or how much damage/interruption it may cause). Calculating risk isn't a cut-and-dried process. While we do our best to be objective in order to make the best use of scarce preparedness resources, there is a large amount of subjectiveness in the process.

. . .

Many ways to calculate risk exist, not all of which are applicable in all cases or at all times. Each particular environment has specific variables that need to be taken into account. The field of risk management has many methods to calculate risk and define risk scores, some of which are quite complex.

A risk management approach uses one of those methods to evaluate hazards/threats. Once done, the the damage they can cause is reduced (mitigated) by putting protection/control measures in place. Mitigation of risk is how a safer environment is created for the congregants.

The resources spent — measured in time, money, and energy — for each environment and each threat should change based on the calculated risk, instead of being driven by current events and emotional responses. It's the emotional, non-calculated approach that has caused so many soft targets around the world to stay that way.

A risk management-based approach to the problem is a real solution that is sustainable.

Some simple formulas

Most of the methods for calculating risk involve some variant of these formulas:

- Risk = Exposure x Hazard
- Risk = Threats x Vulnerabilities

In each, the exposure, hazard, threats, and vulnerabilities are assigned a subjective number, and then those numbers are multiplied to come up with a crude risk score — which then directs the preparedness/mitigation plans.

We've observed that the issues with protecting houses of worship are unique and don't lend themselves easily to such simplistic formulas. We have found it helpful to modify a common risk calculation to take into account those issues and come up with a better risk score.

Background: the CARVER method

CARVER is an acronym that stands for Criticality, Accessibility, Recuperability, Vulnerability, Effect, and Recognizability. The original CARVER method has its origins as a tool for military Special Operations, to help them determine which critical infrastructure targets they needed to destroy to have the greatest impact in a conflict. They wanted to know what would most reliably cause their enemies the greatest amount of damage with a certain level of resources expended.

As the military used this tool to plan war games exercises, they found out that CARVER — which was offensive in nature — could be used by the defending role players to better secure the facilities that were to be "attacked." In their hands, it wasn't a weapon but a defensive strategy tool. It migrated to the rest of the military to be used to secure a wide range of important targets.

When terrorism became a real threat to our critical military facilities, it proved advantageous to add another factor to CARVER: the Shock Factor, which took into account the public perception of an attack on a particular target. This is something terrorists consider when deciding what to attack (and how to attack it).

Over time, this defensive method migrated from the military community to emergency management in general, and is now used as a risk assessment tool for much of our critical infrastructure (such as electrical and communications systems, and our food and fuel supply chains).

Since CARVER+Shock is at its roots a target-based risk assessment tool, it's a great method to use in protecting places of worship. It could benefit from a slight adjustment that recognizes the unique character of religious institutions.

The Place of Worship factor: +P

Because of that unique character, Joshua felt the need to use a risk assessment method that takes into account what makes them unique in our culture. It was an excellent observation; places of worship have to deal with unique obstacles in implementing security plans, and we have to account for that.

Why bother including obstacles to implementation in a risk assessment method? It seems out of place and shouldn't affect the appraisal of the risk from any particular threat. The reason is simple: Our self-made obstacles are risks themselves.

The reluctance to think about security, the lack of desire to face potential harm, and the inevitable arguments about what and how to protect cause places of worship to be more vulnerable than other types of facilities and groups. Some of this is political and some practical, but we doubt there's a congregation where dissent doesn't exist.

These internal obstacles can become large enough that they become a risk to our ability to mitigate threats. Because of this, we feel that this intransigence — which varies from community to community, and even from vulnerability to vulnerability — needs to be a calculated factor. It should have similar planning impact to the other risk indicators. That factor, the Place of Worship factor, is referred to as +P in the CARVER formula.

The result is a method based on the proven risk assessment of CARVER+Shock, but adds in the element that addresses the unique needs of places of worship.

How to use CARVER Risk Assessment

Using any risk assessment method is fairly easy: It's simply a matter of selecting a thing to measure and using a set of standards to evaluate the thing in question.

In our case, the objects we are selecting are the targets (and their environments) that have been identified in previous sections. (Remember, we are including the environments in the list because, as past events have proven, they themselves could be the primary target.)

Once those things are identified, they can be evaluated them against the CARVER scales.

C = Criticality

How valuable is the target/environment to the place of worship? A target is critical when its destruction or damage would significantly impair the ability for it to fulfill its objectives. The sanctuary has high criticality; the parking lot, perhaps not so much.

A = Accessibility

Targets are accessible when a threat can reach the target undetected or unimpeded. Accessibility is the openness of the target to the threat. How easily can the threat get to the target, and how easily can the threat get away? Accessibility includes the ease of gathering intelligence and conducting reconnaissance, in addition to attacking the target and leaving undetected: How easy is it for someone to get the information they need to plan an attack?

R_1 = Recuperability

This is the amount of time, money, or other resources a target needs to recover from damage or destruction by a threat. For intentional threats, a target may not be as appealing if it can be repaired, replaced, or bypassed in a short time with minimal resources.

V = Vulnerability

A target's vulnerability is an overall measurement of the ease with which a target can be damaged or destroyed. If the threat has the means and expertise to conduct the planned attack and the target has weaknesses that would prevent defenses from thwarting the attack, it has a high vulnerability. For non-intentional threats, this includes such things as structural resistance and susceptibility to natural disasters.

E = Effect

Effect refers to the impact, in time and money, to the normal daily functions of the congregation. For instance, an incident could cause a disruption in the food prepared and served to the homeless. If an incident affects the function or productivity, by damage or destruction of a target, it has an effect on the people the institution serves. These effects can include political, economic, legal, and psychological disruption.

. . .

R2 = Recognizability

This is the degree to which a target can be identified by an attacker, without confusion. From the threat's standpoint, the target must be identifiable under various weather and seasonal conditions, in daylight and darkness without being mistaken for other targets. This component is a function of the information (intelligence/reconnaissance) that can be gathered on the target. Can such information be obtained by surveillance, observation, or other means? If so, recognizability is higher than if information is harder to come by.

The +S and +P additions to CARVER: C+S+P

The +S stands for shock — the psychological effects the general public may experience if the target were damaged or destroyed. It measures several factors together, such as psychological and collateral economic impacts of an attack on the target.

While deaths are certainly a big part of the shock factor, human casualties are not required to achieve psychological damage or cause widespread economic loss. The psychological impact is increased when there is a large number of victims, but also when the target has historical, religious, cultural, or other symbolic significance.

The Place of Worship Factor is where we weigh the worship community's resistance to security or risk management efforts. This measurement considers the emotional opposition, the resistance to spending money, the concerns over appearances and impact on traditions, the number of members who are pacifist, and the congregation's overall resistance to change. Some forms of security planning will engender strong feelings of opposition, while others may not cause so much as a raised eyebrow. These should be considered when applying the +P factor.

. . .

Sample scales for each element of the C+S+P risk assessment tool can be found in the appendix, as well as in the separately available workbook (which also contains worksheets and examples of the use of this tool).

Putting it all together: prioritizing risk

Once all the steps in the risk assessment process are completed, the result should be a list of targets and environments that are perceived to be at high risk. Using the relational map that shows which targets could be in which environments, take the individual risk scores identified in the CARVER+S+P exercise and add them to get an overall number.

The resulting score is the overall risk for that specific target and that specific threat. Comparing these numbers is what makes it possible to identify where the targets are the most vulnerable. The higher the score, the more important it is to address the risk.

Combining and separating risk scores

Remember that targets can be within multiple environments, and the target inherits the risk of its environment, increasing their risk score.

Let's say that the minister/priest/rabbi is sitting in his[2] office. His risk score, by itself, may be relatively low. But what if the administration building he's in has a higher score? His risk is now the same as the building, which means his risk score has increased simply by where he happens to be. The environment modifies his risk score.

This is why soft targets are so dangerous. An otherwise undesirable or uninteresting (from an attacker's point of view) target, going into a desirable environment, can be at dramatically increased risk. A brand new priest, one whom no one knows and who has yet to take any controversial positions, may by himself have a low risk. But he becomes a high-risk target when he's transferred into a high-risk parish — even though he's not yet done anything to raise his personal risk level.

If all the targets are in a building and the building has the highest risk score, everything in the building would have the same score. In such a case, it is clear the outer environments that have been identified need to be on the list of risks to be mitigated.

The problem is that the overwhelming risk of that environment can mask vulnerabilities underneath, vulnerabilities that should be addressed. Although this situation is rare, if it does occur simply exclude the environmental score to make the underlying vulnerabilities more obvious.

Reason over emotion

Once the targets are sorted from high to low by their risk scores, go back and look at the original threat assessments again, paying attention to the kinds of likely incidents.

Many who do place-of-worship security tend to assign risk priority based on whatever the hot-button issue is at the time. Again, we typically see this in the aftermath of an active killer incident, which might be anywhere in the country (or even the world).

It's very easy to get sidetracked by the scariest threats, or those with the greatest media attention, but the reality is that not everything is equally likely. Pay attention to those that are more plausible, that could realistically happen.

Combined with the risk scoring, the highest priority targets/incidents should be clear. Those will guide the mitigation/response planning.

Spending an afternoon on the shooting range isn't a measured protective response. Neither is a cursory walk through the building with an alarm system salesperson. Without a solid understanding of what needs to be protected, what dangers they face, and what the likely incidents might be, it's almost impossible to give the community any real protection.

When a "top 10" or "top 20" list of targets and incidents has been made, and there are clear and demonstrable reasons why they are in that particular order, then there is something on which to base the protective and mitigation activities.

RISK MITIGATION PLANNING

Risk mitigation is reducing the severity or impact of any specific threat, based on the particular vulnerabilities of any given target. Mitigation is the planning, preparation, and response that reduce the likelihood of an incident that impacts the worship community, or reducing its effect if it does happen.

Mitigation is everything from installing fire extinguishers to team members responding to an active shooter. It includes fire alarms and first aid training, executive protection for clergy, and seismic retrofitting to guard against earthquake damage. It even includes insurance coverage and calling 911.

It's far less effective, however, when congregations start mitigation without knowing what, why, or how they should be approaching the problem.

Reaction instead of response

It's all too common for people to jump into mitigation efforts based on what they feel, rather than what they actually know. This often happens in the aftermath of a well-publicized attack on a group or institution, regardless of the methods or motives of the attackers. The more brazen or severe the attack, the more likely it is to capture the attention of people in worship communities. The "threat of the day" becomes the impetus to put plans into place.

There's a big problem with this emotion-based approach to risk management: Whatever is in the news drives the planning, which in turn eats up preparedness resources (time, energy, attention, and money). Regardless of how likely or unlikely that same attack is on any given community, all the preparedness resources are spent and nothing is left over for more common, likely, and just as lethal threats.

This is why formal risk management — assessing targets, threats, and vulnerabilities — is so important. Without it, it's not possible to rationally decide which or how much of the available mitigation resources should be spent on any given threat scenario. It's not possible to accurately gauge which risks are more important to prepare for, and which are less so.

Making decisions without the information from the preceding chapter means constantly reacting (emotionally) to every perceived threat, rather than responding (rationally) to what is known to be valid for the congregation.

Avoiding the hard sell

Whenever a "crisis du jour" happens, opportunists come out of the woodwork. Firearms instructors, martial arts instructors, alarm companies, and others sense fear in the market, fear that they can exploit for their own financial gain. What they fail to tell their potential customers is that a security person with a gun doesn't instantly make a soft target a hardened target, nor does an alarm system, camera system, or knowing judo.

As a mutual friend of the authors recently quipped, "Being prepared starts in your head, not your holster." The challenge in keeping houses of worship the safe havens they should be goes far beyond any one issue or any one threat.

As the old saying goes: "If all you have is a hammer, every problem looks like a nail." Amateurs look to mitigate a single risk using the limited knowledge and skill they have. Risk management professionals find ways to mitigate all the important risks.

When we talk about hardening our soft targets like places of worship, we can't take a single risk, mitigate it, and call it done. Intuitive risk mitigation will never adequately convert soft targets to hard targets. It takes quantification and prioritization based on a value to harden soft targets. It's narrow minded and reckless to think otherwise.

What is at stake here is human life. The responsible approach to risk mitigation should be the professional approach. It is our moral responsibility to do this to the best of our abilities. The goal is to make soft targets evolve into hard targets, resistant to damage.

If the information collected up to this point has been well prepared and analyzed, there should now exist a priority-based list of targets with data to back up the conclusions. That fact-based, reason-based list is what's used to put safeguards and countermeasures in place.

. . .

Dealing with risk

The risks identified and ranked for each target can be addressed in any of four ways:

- *Reduce:* Put safeguards into place that protect the target's vulnerabilities. Risk reduction generally falls to detection, delay, and response functions. Examples are smoke alarms to detect fire, bars on windows to delay intruder entry, and trained security to respond to an active attack.
- *Transfer:* Allow or require someone else to accept the risk and mitigate the resulting damage. The most obvious example is insurance, where the risk is borne by the company in exchange for money (premiums). Less obvious examples are police agencies, military forces, and fire departments. *Important note: While risk can be transferred, responsibility cannot. The congregation may have insurance against people slipping on entry walkways, but that doesn't relieve the responsibility to put down salt to melt the ice and prevent the accident.*
- *Avoid:* Make changes that reduce the chance of encountering the threat. This might involve changing venues, moving a vulnerable target, or modifying a process to eliminate the cause of the risk. Not walking through a high-crime area at night is an example of avoidance.
- *Accept:* A strategic decision to do nothing to reduce the risk. There are some risks whose likelihood is so low, or whose consequence is so minimal, that they're not worth expending the congregation's limited preparedness resources (time, money, and/or effort). A petty theft is something that might be absorbed as an operating cost rather than spending multiple thousands of dollars to prevent. Other threats may be so unlikely that it doesn't make sense to divert resources from other, more likely and more damaging, threat preparedness. Risk acceptance is not always a bad thing. If done carefully, it can be a good tool to help allocate resources properly.

As the Safety Council decides on which approach is best for any given threat, and starts to consider safeguards and countermeasures, it's important to understand that it's not possible to mitigate all risk. As long as the world contains things of value, there will always be targets. Those targets will always have some vulnerability, and there will always be threats looking to exploit those vulnerabilities. Although risk cannot be reduced to zero, it can be reduced to an acceptable level.

That, in a nutshell, is what risk management is all about.

Which approach is best?

For each target and each threat, a decision on how to manage the risk (chosen from the four approaches above) is needed.

There's really no work to acceptance; once that route is chosen, the work is finished. Avoidance, on the other hand, is more of a pre-determined tactical (event-based) decision than a strategic plan. With regards to transference, most of the transfer of risk already exists in the form of insurance and pre-planned decisions to call 911 for situations that go beyond the congregation's abilities.

In reality, most risk mitigation work is focused on reducing vulnerabilities. Reduction through detection, delay, and response will likely be the best choice for many (if not most) of the threats that have been identified. This is where most of the community's time, money, and energy will be spent.

Reducing vulnerabilities

"Desperation, weakness, vulnerability -- these things will always be exploited. You need to protect the weak, ring-fence them, with something far stronger than empathy." -- Zadie Smith

. . .

Before going too far into the process of mitigating vulnerabilities, the Safety Council will have to consider where to draw the line. The congregation's preparedness resources — time, money, energy (labor), and even interest — are all limited. Because of that, it's just not possible to prepare for everything. Decisions need to be made about what risks will get attention, of what kind and how much, and which might need to remain unaddressed (the acceptance approach). This is called resource allocation.

When evaluating threats and risks for resource allocation, it's useful to ask two questions for each one:

- *What's the scope of this task?* This is where preparedness resources are considered. How much will it cost? How much time will it take? How much labor and how many people need to be involved? Hard estimates aren't necessarily needed at this point, but the tasks should at least be divided into high, medium, and low categories for each of those resources.
- *What is the risk appetite?* This is the amount of risk the congregation — represented by both the clergy and the lay leadership — is willing to accept. For instance, the congregation may have a high risk appetite for graffiti vandalism, if prevention means spending tens of thousands of dollars in surveillance equipment and monitoring. Another example might be the congregation accepting the small possibility of an active killer type of attack rather than accepting armed security personnel in their sanctuary.

Be aware that risk appetite is not static or constant; it often changes when facts are presented. Many worship communities take the ostrich approach (head in the sand) to threats and vulnerabilities, yet when presented with a full risk assessment, the collective attitude changes. People with good hearts sometimes pause when they realize their willingness to accept risk is different than their willingness to accept the consequences of that decision.

It's important to have this discussion with the decision makers in the congregation. It's important to determine their risk appetite and not push beyond it. This is a grave responsibility, as pushing too far may derail the entire process.

Deciding on appropriate safeguards

For any given target, there may be more than one way of reducing its vulnerabilities. However, it's one thing to identify a list of safeguards. It's an entirely different task to identify the correct safeguard, the one that is effective and falls within the available resources and the expected risk appetite.

It's important to recognize that not all safeguards are equal. Some simply do a better job of reducing the risks towards a target. The overriding concern, the first criteria, should be that of effectiveness. The correct safeguard is generally the most effective one.

In Josh's consulting work, he noticed that some groups struggle to compare safeguards and decide which one is more effective. In some cases, this causes very spirited discussions among proponents of each safeguard! To help facilitate the discussion, he created a simple framework that allows the comparison of safeguards based on which mitigation elements it satisfies. It's called the Safeguard Effectiveness Matrix.

This can be done using a piece of paper or a spreadsheet. List each safeguard under consideration, and make five columns labeled Identify, Detect, Delay, Respond, and Assess:

- **Identify:** Does the safeguard give the means to identify possible threats prior to an attack on the target? Being able to classify possible threats as potential threats due to markers or "red flags" makes it easier to devise more specific safeguards.
- **Detect:** Does the safeguard allow detection of a threat prior to it actually harming a target? A person in an observation tower watching over an area can detect the potential threat of a person walking toward the perimeter, but a person with binoculars can spot the details and identify if the person is truly a threat. The goal of detection is specificity, as opposed to labeling everything a threat and adopting a blanket approach to protection.
- **Delay:** Does the safeguard prevent or slow access to the target? Door locks, speed bumps, and access control are all safeguards that delay access to a target.
- **Respond:** Can someone or something intervene before the threat reaches its intended target? A first responder, armed or unarmed, may intercept an attacker before he can reach his intended target. An automated system, such as a fire alarm, can summon the fire department.
- **Assess:** Is there a method of verifying that safeguards are functioning and have not been compromised? Setting up a motion-activated camera allows verification that access has been restricted after hours to a particular area. If that camera is activated during restricted hours, you know there has been a breach of access.

Put a check in each column where the safeguard satisfies the mitigation element(s). The more checkmarks, the more effective the safeguard is relative to the other safeguards.

Hardening targets and environments

The idea of hardening — also known as fortifying — is just one general category of safeguard, but it's important enough to consider on its own. Fortification is a fundamental protection strategy and the mechanics could fill a book on their own, but we'd like to bring attention to hardening as a ***concept***.

To fortify something is to put preventive and protective safeguards in place to protect it. In fortifying a building, for instance, those safeguards might include shatter-resistant glass, fire sprinklers, and bollards (metal/concrete posts designed to impede vehicular attacks). Safeguards can be in or around the building, but the key is that they have the property of physically protecting the building from damage or intrusion.

That's the minimal requirement to harden a target, and it's as far as most institutions go. To fully harden a target, there must two additional things: a safeguard of last resort, and a counterintelligence element. The latter will be covered in another section; here, we're going to consider what we call the safeguard of last resort.

When we harden a target, we strengthen it. There is no doubt that preventive and protective safeguards strengthen our target. But what happens if all of those protective layers are breached or compromised? That's where the safeguard of last resort comes in.

No other options

Our law enforcement officers have them; they wear them every day. Police officers have many safeguards in place to protect themselves so they can continue to protect the public, including their radios, with which they can call for help; and their ballistic vests, which stop bullets, knives, and even help prevent injuries during an automobile accident.

But they have one tool that is activated only when everything else has failed: their duty pistol. When they have no options and all their safe-guards have been compromised, they depend on that safeguard of last resort to keep them alive.

It is important for us to build safeguards of last resort into our mitigation strategy for places of worship. These safeguards are job-specific, meaning they perform a specific task against a specific kind of threat.

What would the safeguard of last resort be for an armed attack on the congregation? This is the proper place for members who are lawfully armed, but perhaps not part of a First Responder Team. Those armed members need to understand their place in the process of protection: They are not the first responders, but rather people who may be expected to respond if the first responder team fails to gain control of the situation.

A good method of dealing with armed congregants is to accept that they're armed, as long as the condition for allowing them to be so armed on the property is that they understand their role as safeguards of last resort and that they're coordinated with the First Responder Team(s).

Audit controls

Part of ensuring the effectiveness of a safeguard is auditing its function. Automated controls break, humans make mistakes, technology has bugs, and sometimes things just don't do what we expect them to. Auditing gives the control tool to ensure that safeguards are doing what they're supposed to do. *Auditing safeguards is just as important as putting the safeguards in place.*

Each safeguard has its own set of audit criteria, and those for one congregation won't necessarily be the same as a congregation on the other side of town. What's more, the audit process used to track a fire alarm system is different than that used to audit a First Responder Team.

Audit criteria are always unique

It's important that the audit criteria and process be developed from scratch to fit the congregation; this is not a place to take shortcuts. A mistake we often see is either using a generic "one size fits all" checklist, or borrowing a checklist that someone else created.

By nature, a generic checklist can't possibly go into the details of what needs to be tested at every place of worship. At the same time, borrowing from a checklist that someone else created for their specific place of worship can lead to missing critical pieces or missing something unique. A great example of this happened when Josh began working with his former church to setup a First Responder Team.

One of his first tasks was to do the yearly security and safety audit. This was typically done using a checklist that had been given to one of the church leaders by a member of a church in a different town. The checklist had been in use for a few years and was held as an example of due care.

On the checklist was a section for checking fire extinguishers. According to the checklist, it was necessary to verify that the extinguisher was still in place, verify the pressure was showing within the acceptable range, and verify that the inspection tag was not out of date.

For the church that donated the checklist, it was perfect. They had simple firefighting needs, and all of their extinguishers were of the same dry ABC chemical type. The problem was that Josh's home church had a variety of electronic equipment which demanded CO_2 type extinguishers. As it turned out, the wrong extinguishers had been placed in some locations; it wasn't obvious to others, but Josh's technology background led him to spot the error.

After investigating, it was discovered that they'd been placed in the wrong locations after they were inspected a few years earlier. It turns out that a member of the church had gathered up the extinguishers and took them to the servicing company to have them inspected; upon returning them, he simply hung them on their hooks without regard for which went where, because that information wasn't on the checklist. In the ensuing years subsequent people just checked off the boxes on the form, not knowing that the CO_2 extinguishers meant for the electronics room had been swapped with a different and unsuitable type.

This is a simple yet real-life example of why an audit checklist needs to be specific to the place of worship if it is to be effective.

Don't take shortcuts

The temptation to find shortcuts in the audit process will be strong, but the integrity of the security plan demands that the Safety Council make the effort to audit regularly and thoroughly. The audit controls need to be based on the safeguards put in place in their house of worship, not somewhere else.

List each safeguard and list ways to verify that it's functioning properly. Make periodic checks of those controls, as well as a regular formal audit to verify everything is in place. Any findings should be noted and plans to correct them should be outlined. They should be reviewed in Safety Council meetings until they are resolved.

We are aware of many security breaches that would likely not have occurred had an audit process been put in place. We don't know if the system is working unless it's checked periodically!

Financial considerations

As we've previously mentioned, the cost of security is a major obstacle to protecting places of worship. We've also discussed that one of the ways to deal with this obstacle is to present a comprehensive plan that carefully considers the costs involved in the mitigation of risk.

Even with that being done, there will always be the matter of convincing the skeptical that the proposed actions, and the money spent, really will result in risk reduction. We suggest taking a hard look at the highest cost items. To be financially viable, they need to result in the greatest reduction of risk. If they don't, they'll be very hard to sell to the people who control the purse strings.

Carefully present the plan and outline the costs, ensuring that all the in the proposal have been identified. Here are some examples of costs that should be included:

- Acquisition: what it costs to purchase the safeguard outright (hardware and equipment)
- Lease/rental: many security items are leased or rented, and this is a recurring (ongoing) cost
- Installation: putting the safeguard into place and making it operational
- Operation: the expense of actually using the safeguard

- Maintenance: include both regular (scheduled) maintenance and expected repairs
- Training: what it costs to properly instruct people how to use the safeguard effectively
- Standby: costs not otherwise accounted for, when the safeguard isn't actively being used

This level of detail and rigor is necessary to show the skeptics there are no surprises. Showing all the costs, along with the expected benefits that outweigh the expenses, should convince any reasonable person that the project is worth doing.

Being patient, understanding, and respectful will go a long way toward breaking down the resistance that keeps the congregation from implementing a serious risk mitigation plan.

TRAINING PEOPLE TO RESPOND

The best risk management plan is useless without some sort of response function. Whether it's immediate medical care or intruder interdiction, response to an incident is necessary to safeguard the well-being of the targets. This means deciding what needs to be done and who will do it, then teaching people what to do, when to do it, and how to do it. This process forms the basis of responder training.

The largest portion of any risk mitigation plan needs to be plans to train people in how to respond properly. These people include any First Responder Teams, the worship leadership, and even the congregation as a whole.

Training and practice

Training, as we use the word, is the learning of or exposure to new skills. Skills aren't learned in just one session; the learned skills need to be rehearsed in order to make them useful, and to make them usable without notice. This rehearsal process is called practice: the deliberate, repeated exercise of a skill in order to build proficiency.

. . .

Everyone needs both training and practice in order to gain competency and confidence in their skills. Training and practice are both long-term commitments and often overlooked in risk management plans. This ongoing cycle of training and practice needs to be provided for in the overall risk mitigation planning.

Understand that training or practice aren't always major events or involved affairs. Practice can be as simple as an informal drill every so often. But this doesn't mean those drills shouldn't be planned! The only ways to make sure practice happens are to schedule it and have a way to track that the practice sessions actually happened.

Practice sessions also provide valuable feedback as to how good the initial training is. It may become apparent that certain skills aren't being learned, or that the skills proved inadequate in some way and need to be retrained.

If the training is to be handled in-house, the designated instructors will need training not only in the skills they'll be teaching, but also in the art and science of teaching itself. The best practitioner in the world will be an ineffective instructor if he can't teach others how to do what he does. This, too, needs to be accounted for in the risk management plans.

It should be clearer that training is indeed a huge part of risk management. Don't overlook or try to short-change the training and practice cycle.

Who and what to train

Not everyone needs to be trained to do the same job, and not everyone needs to know precisely how others are trained. People need to be trained according to what they'll be expected to do and in consideration of their interests and abilities.

If it's decided to task the First Responder Teams with security duties, their training should include de-escalation techniques, first aid and trauma response; if they're armed, they'll also need some specific and well-practiced shooting skills. And that's the bare minimum! They'll also benefit from training in unarmed defensive skills, as well as practice in diplomacy and "customer service."

Scenario training

Scenario-based training (SBT) is one of the most effective ways to both train and evaluate skills. It can also be used as a test device for the risk plan itself, and to evaluate both the student and the teacher. Scenario-based training is a subset of a larger training concept known as reality-based training (RBT).

As the name implies, SBT involves setting up scenarios (incidents) and then having participants role-play all parties, from initiation through response. The object is to test how well the participants handle an evolving event, including carefully controlled variables.

Scenario-based training usually involves these components:

- Elements: specific people, in their specific roles, who would be present in the specific incident
- Circumstances: the reason for the incident happening, or the interactions that initiate the incident
- Environments: the physical locations or features, if they're important to the incident

Scenarios recreate circumstances that have happened, or could happen, between the elements in the environment being recreated.

The defining characteristic of scenario-based training is the interaction between the elements (people) involved. In a scenario involving a criminal attack, it's about the interactions between the attacker(s) and defender(s); in a non-intentional scenario, it's the interactions between victims and the responders that are important.

In all cases, it's the responses that are being tested.

Realistic or authentic?

It's possible to set up a scenario of a hostage rescue team storming an aircraft. People have actually built mock-ups of airliner interiors in warehouses, complete with seats and dummies in those seats. The whole scene is very authentic, in that it recreates a specific environment in sufficient detail to make the role players feel as though they're really in that environment.

But to have value to the participants, the scene must be *realistic*: it must recreate an environment that is relevant to the participants in just enough detail that they can recognize it as being relevant. The most authentic recreation isn't realistic if the environment being recreated isn't one the participants spend time in. Realism is dependent on the lives of the participants.

It's possible, therefore, to be very authentic but not very realistic. The reverse is also true: It's possible to be quite realistic without necessarily being all that authentic. If the environment has meaning to the participants, even if the recreation is on the abstract side, it will be realistic to the role players.

. . .

Many people who put on scenario training spend a lot of time, energy, and money making them authentic — to accurately recreate an environment from *someone's* life — when they really need to be realistic: to recreate an environment from the *role players'* lives.

This goes for the circumstances as well. In order to be realistic, the scenario must recreate events that are relevant to the participants. In the case of protecting houses of worship, a scenario involving police chasing down an armed robber probably isn't relevant. The people involved are different, their roles relative to each other are different, and their interactions are going to be different.

Unless the people running the training are very careful, and the people seeking that training are very discerning, it's easy for things to get out of hand and turn into authentic entertainment instead of realistic training.

Where to find scenario-based training

In recent years, many reality-based training facilities have sprung up to cater to the burgeoning demand for "tactical" training. They usually feature reconfigurable buildings or sets in which they can mock up environments, with widely varying degrees of authenticity.

Most of these facilities focus on firearms training. Their facilities are designed primarily to be used with modified firearms that shoot small paint capsules (marker rounds) or plastic BBs at low velocities. While not necessarily lethal, they do present an injury hazard, and protective clothing and gear must be worn.

. . .

Some also have impact-protective suits available, which allow role players to safely hit each other with impact weapons such as batons.

This kind of training can, if properly run, be very valuable — but is does have downsides. First, it's very easy to get caught up in the authenticity of the created environment (some have fully furnished rooms, down to such things as vases of flowers on bookcases) and forget all about the necessary realism.

Second, this kind of training facility is also expensive to use. The amount of time and money spent in setting up a shooting range that is both configurable and safe is considerable, and they typically sit unused a great deal of the time. As a result, the hourly expense is high.

Third, these facilities often don't have anyone on staff who is conversant with all possible environments and circumstances, so the participants are often forced to provide their own exercise coordinator who develops the scenarios and scripts. This person is usually (but not always) the instructor who oversees the scenario and interprets the results in a way to help the participants learn. If he/she isn't well versed in the unique demands of reality-based training, then the exercises can easily become worthless.

Finally, this kind of live-fire training can be exceedingly dangerous. While the marker rounds aren't themselves necessarily deadly, serious injuries due to lack of safety gear have occurred. They become more when there is a lack of proper safety protocols and lax enforcement of them. Many people have been killed when live ammunition somehow made its way into a scenario where only marker rounds were supposed to have been used. This happens at all levels of training; one of the authors lived in a county where the local SWAT team accidentally killed one of its own members in such a training exercise.

· · ·

Doing it yourself

As noted, this type of training facility is rare and expensive to use. We recognize that many congregations are unable to avail themselves of the use of a reality-based training facility. It's possible, though, to do this kind of training in any place of worship using inert or prop guns; in the trade, they're called "blue guns," and are solid rubber replicas that do not fire a projectile.

Yes, they do take away much of the authenticity of a scenario, yet if the scenario is constructed properly, they can still provide great feedback. In fact, it may be better to start the scenario training in this way and then move on to the RBT facility.

Non-firearms scenarios are very easy to set up in almost any sanctuary, and in fact are probably best done there.

The "bible" of reality-based training is the book *Training At The Speed Of Life* by Kenneth Murray. We strongly recommend that the people in charge of training response teams have and read this book before engaging in any RBT — even if it's to be conducted by professionals at a dedicated training facility.

Making scenario training useful

In order to have value, the scenarios need to be plausible. They need to reflect an event that could reasonably be expected to happen in or to the worship community. In other words, they need to be realistic in terms of the people participating, and they need to reflect the kinds of incidents identified in the assessment process.

· · ·

Once a plausible scenario has been selected, a script of the attack is developed — a script that reflects the incident accurately. This script guides the role players, but may not be revealed to the people under test (the defenders).

The people chosen to play the roles of the antagonists (attackers) need to stick closely to the script, because the purpose of scenario training is to teach or evaluate responses, and in order to do that, there has to be a constant stimulus. That constant is the attack script.

Role players must be chosen who will take the process seriously and stick to the script. It does no one any good, and it's not safe, to have a Rambo-wannabe running through the scenario, rolling across the ground and spraying paint rounds everywhere.

It's also important to limit the ratio of firearms-related incidents to the actual frequency of occurrence. Remember that the active shooter attack occurs rarely, even though they get the vast majority of media attention. The number of shooting incidents in the scenario training should happen in proper proportion to the other kinds of incidents.

Fire drills are a kind of scenario training and should be done regularly. Severe weather events, medical emergencies, belligerent visitors, and more should show up in scenario training as often as — or more often than — shooting incidents. Don't limit scenarios to firearms, because not all problems are solved with firearms.

Testing the plans

It has been said that no plan survives first contact with the enemy. That is not an excuse to dismiss the planning, however! As one of

Grant's acquaintances — an Air Force colonel — once told him, "Without a plan, you don't know where the deviations are going to occur."

Scenario training is a chance to identify those deviations and refine the plans. That is why the professionals go to elaborate means to test their plans in advance of needing to use them. When plans are tested against a determined human adversary, that's when the problems, the deviations, begin to appear. From that experience can be made changes which bring the plans closer to reality.

In the case of worship security, the plans made from the careful target, threat, and risk assessments should essentially be a set of safeguards to intercept an attack at the earliest point where it can be prevented (or limited in the damage it causes). Those safeguards will look great on paper, yet until they're tested, no one will know if they'll work under the stress of an incident.

Inducing stress

In order for this type of training to be effective, it needs to produce a level of manageable stress in the participants. This doesn't mean to overwhelm them and force them to fail; that approach is far too common in the training world, and it's damaging to the learning process.

The more effective approach is to start the participants at a level of complexity and stress where they can perform successfully. Once they understand both the plan/script and the training process, the difficulty can be increased. The scenario can unfold more quickly; unforeseen problems or obstacles may begin to appear.

.   .   .

If this process is done properly, the participants will develop a sense of confidence. They'll begin to feel they can handle that type of incident, even if the unexpected occurs. That's exactly what we want to happen!

Alternatives to scenario training

Scenario training is a superb way to develop and test response skills, but it's not always an option. The resources and facilities are not always available for this type of training.

In those cases, we suggest doing what are known as tabletop exercises. We see these often in the movies: good guys or bad guys have models of their targets or objectives, and they rehearse what each person is going to do at specific times. These kinds of exercises start acquainting the participants with their tasks and responses in a low-pressure way and enable them to see the totality of the incident.

There are various ways to do tabletop exercises, and the best way to integrate them into the training process is to hire someone familiar with the process to coordinate the training, which will then be facilitated by in-house personnel. If the budget is tight, local fire departments can often facilitate or offer training in how to put together such exercises, often at little to no cost.

Some emergency management agencies also provide training, but in our experience the quality varies rather considerably. Fire departments do such exercises routinely and are generally pretty good at it.

It's useful to get law enforcement, the fire department, and perhaps even local Homeland Security representatives involved in these exercises. They will have insight into how they might approach these incidents, and the junction points where the in-house responders might interact with theirs during an incident. In our experience, this has proven to be extremely valuable for all sides.

Training the entire congregation

One of the best tests of any first responder plan is to try it out with a large sample of the people who would be in the environment in which the incident would occur. There is, we've found, no better way to understand the chaos and unpredictability of a room full of people than to ask them what they would do in a particular situation and note how many different — and sometimes contradictory — answers are offered.

Some people may run for the exits, others may try to hide, others may jump up and scream, still others may run around with their hands flailing in the air looking for someone to protect them. Some people who have had no interest in security or defense up to that point will become heroic, rushing the attacker and taking grievous wounds.

It is also possible to encounter people who, despite being untrained and unprepared, try to force their way into a position of authority. Knowing this is possible, and training for such possibilities, is valuable in refining the response plans.

Tell members what's expected

Most people want to be told what to do in these situations. Training with a large group of congregants allows them to learn what they're expected to do. There will always be a few who will buck the system, but the majority have no clue what they need to do and would prefer that someone just tell them.

. . .

As the response plans come together, consider what the congregation at large might be expected to do for each kind of incident. Document that and share it during these training sessions. Done properly, this can really ease the minds of those who are worried about threats to the worship community. Knowing that the group is prepared for all types of incidents is a comfort to many people.

Keep the participant groups small until the responses have been refined and the first responders have become comfortable with their jobs. At that point, invite as many people as practical to participate.

We stress that these sessions should always be by invitation only. Don't be discouraged if participation isn't great the first time. Keep offering, and more people will begin to show up. It might be surprising how people's interest changes as they become more comfortable with the idea and wanting to know what they can do to help.

A note about operational security: *Be extremely cautious about who gets invited to these events. Don't allow new members, visitors, or those who may be considered potential threats to participate in these events. If someone does show up uninvited, this may be a strong indicator of a pending attack.*

After Action Reviews

The term After Action Review (AAR) originated in the military. After the completion of a military action or training session, a review is conducted. The goal of the AAR is to learn from both successes and mistakes in training and on the battlefield, so that soldiers can become a stronger and more experienced fighting force. The institutionalization of AARs over the years has matured our military immensely. It's shaped the way they conduct operations and the way they train.

. . .

AARs have migrated from the military to all kinds of response operations and activities. Grant has facilitated and participated in both formal and informal AARs in search-and-rescue operations and emergency communications exercises, while Joshua has lead AARs after business continuity and disaster recovery tests, executive protection details, and "red team" (real-time intrusion test) engagements. Both of us feel that they're invaluable to the training and progression of any response function.

An AAR is a time to reflect and ask the hard questions: What went wrong? Even after a successful mission, things that could have been done better are always identified. This process of continuous improvement makes a response team a more refined and fluid group.

An AAR is also a time to learn how people on the First Responder Team think. Each person has different backgrounds, experiences, and personalities, as well as different strengths and weaknesses. By going through the AAR process, everyone begins to learn why the team zigged instead of zagged.

The review lets everyone involved learn to play to their strengths and develop a level of trust that allows them to make decisions without question. The AAR is key to developing that bond in a team, and between the team and its supervisors.

The goal is to improve responses and develop a cohesive team. There should be a moderator who keeps people on track and guides participants into asking relevant questions, but checklists about what to review aren't necessarily needed. An AAR can simply be a mental "walk through" of the training event or operational incident. Done in a step-by-step methodology, and focused on improvement rather than bureaucratic fault-finding, everyone will find value in the process.

. . .

The role of worship leaders

In the religions and denominations the authors are familiar with, the worship leaders — be they actual clergy or laypeople — are usually seated (or stand) at the front of the congregation. Many times they're facing the congregation, meaning they can see areas the congregants can't. Since sanctuaries are often set up with the entrances at the rear of the room, the worship leaders are able to see newcomers (and late-comers), and may even be able to see the foyer or vestibule where people are entering the building.

Due to their unique physical position, worship leaders are able to see problems as they develop. They may have the first warning of an unfolding attack, and most importantly, they can see everyone in the sanctuary. Body language is an important component of detecting hostility, and the leaders are likely to see it before anyone else.

Because of this, they should be trained in both spotting the red flags of a developing incident and in ways to alert the security responders that something requires their attention. There should be a discreet way for the leaders to alert security personnel of a problem, of what nature, and its approximate location without panicking everyone in the building.

Hospitals have code terms they can broadcast over the PA system to tell staff there's a problem and where it is, without the patients and visitors being aware. Something similar should be worked out with worship leaders and security personnel. These codes and responses should be practiced occasionally so everyone knows how to use them and what they mean.

. . .

If traditions allow it and the architecture is amenable, consider mounting a monitored security camera to see from the worship leader's position. It may be the best early warning vantage point to be had in many buildings.

WHAT ABOUT WORSHIP SECURITY TEAMS?

Whenever the topic of security in houses of worship comes up, the talk almost invariably centers on the idea of security teams: groups of congregants, very often armed, whose responsibility is to keep the worshippers safe from attackers during services.

As we hope we've made clear in the rest of this book, security teams aren't the only component of an effective protection plan. In fact, they're probably not even the most important. More important are understanding the congregation's threats and vulnerabilities, and understanding how to meet the challenges they present.

The congregation may decide a security team is a necessary part of their plan, but the plan should determine the need for the team — not the other way around. Assessments and planning, if done honestly and thoroughly, will indicate whether a security team is right for the community.

. . .

This is partly why we've adopted the term First Responder Team, rather than "security team". Keeping the congregation safe requires a more comprehensive approach than just carrying a gun and shooting people.

Issues with "security teams"

At the beginning of this book, we noted an increase in what we see as "militarization" of houses of worship. Whenever a mass-casualty attack happens anywhere in this country, regardless of the target of the attack, congregations everywhere start talking about forming armed, roving teams. Emphasis is placed on learning to shoot and carrying weapons, with very little (if any) thought given to identifying and mitigating all the other risks the congregation may face.

This is a troubling trend. While we applaud the dedication and earnestness of people who want to keep the members of their worship community safe, honesty compels us to point out that they're preparing for a very narrow range of security threats. Not only are they often focused on one relatively rare subset of possible threats, but they also tend to be outward-looking and sometimes oblivious to the threats posed by their own congregants.

These teams often (usually, in fact) end up in charge of the congregation's entire security posture. This is problematic on several levels.

Lack of community involvement

A big issue is the inherent isolation of the security team. Only those people who are interested in the kind of "hands-on" activities they tend to do will join. This is usually a very small percentage of the congregation and tends to skew heavily male.

. . .

When the security team is also the de-facto leadership in security and preparedness planning for the entire worship community, this exclusivity deprives the group of valuable insight and intelligence. In extreme cases, it can result in a lack of broad support for the group's mission among the rest of the congregation.

This can be avoided by placing the security teams under the umbrella of the Safety Council, whose members are intentionally drawn from a wide swath of the congregation. Their primary jobs are planning and intelligence gathering. The security components of a First Responder Team, if a need is both identified and felt, can then be recruited from those congregants interested in their specialized duty.

Dangers of unchecked delegation

We've seen congregations whose entire approach to safety was to hire a uniformed security company. No planning, no forethought, not even an introduction so the security officers could meet the members they were to "protect." The security companies often have no knowledge of the nature and unique characteristics of the congregation they're supposed to serve.

What's more, in these cases the entire responsibility for the safety of the community has usually been placed in the company's hands; all security concerns delegated to them. After all, they were being paid to do the job! That's where the congregation's participation in their own security ended.

This isn't just an issue with paid security services, either. We see the same thing with homegrown security teams. When a team is formed, it seems natural for the congregational leadership to delegate all responsibility and decision-making to them. Congregational safety is a complex and sometimes scary thing to confront, and it's easy to allow a small, unaccountable team to take over that function.

As a result, the team is often left to self-govern with little or no oversight from either the lay leaders or clergy. Out of sight, out of mind. The group dynamic leads them to stand apart from their fellow congregants, and over time this can cause the team to have an unhealthy, elitist view of themselves and their position.

It's dangerous when a security apparatus, whether secular or religious, begins to think of itself in those terms. When a small group of people holds themselves above others, abuses begin. Those abuses may be subtle or overt, but are always a possibility. Resentment among their fellow congregants may fester, undermining both their ability to protect others and the congregation's ability to maintain a stable and righteous security posture.

Keeping the team focused on service

The authors are united in their dislike of referring to any security team as a "ministry." We recognize this may be a controversial position to take, but the term is too often used to set some people apart from and above others. This is a dangerous road to travel with security personnel. The dangers of abuse of power, either real or perceived, are too great. Putting that temptation in front of them is, we feel, morally wrong.

Instead, we suggest that security volunteers always be referred to in relatively neutral terms, which is why we've adopted the term First Responder Team. We would go so far as to say that the ideal candidate for a position on a security team would be the person who sees him or herself as a servant to others, as opposed to someone who looks on the position as a means of gaining status or as a way to show off his tactical training.

Part of the task of forming a team is thoroughly screening those who want to join, to ensure they have the proper attitude toward the task.

Safety and security aren't things to delegate away, regardless of whether the functions are assigned to paid professionals or allowed to be taken over by people within the worship community. The community needs to retain control to ensure their security is done in a manner that's congruent with both their religious tradition and their moral foundation.

The solution is to bring these functions into the open. Make sure a wide range of personalities, backgrounds, and interests are involved in the congregation's security planning. The security team should be a part of the Safety Council, and their functions regularly reviewed.

Legalities of security teams

Neither of the authors is a lawyer, and what follows is *not* legal advice.

When worship security teams are formed, often little thought is given to the legalities and liabilities involved. In most states, professional security services must be licensed, bonded, and insured. If the security officers carry firearms, there is usually additional training and certification that must be obtained.

While a volunteer security team may not seem to be required to do these things, it's important to understand the precise legal requirements in their state and municipality to know for sure. Depending on the letter of the law and the court decisions, any formal or organized group may fall under the statutes governing for-profit security services.

If the deciding factor is compensation, understand that almost anything can be considered payment for services rendered. Does the congregation pay for their training or equipment? Are they provided radios or food? Who pays for the inevitably necessary liability insurance? These things all need to be taken into account, as any might be construed as compensation under certain circumstances.

Another issue concerns the presence of firearms in a house of worship. In some states, a person with a concealed carry license is allowed to carry a firearm almost anywhere, including a house of worship. In other states, carrying a firearm in a religious building is allowed only with the permission of the pastor, minister, priest, rabbi, or board of directors.

As this is written, two states prohibit the carrying of firearms in houses of worship but have an exemption for members of a security team. However, they require extra or specialized training, along with written notification to the rest of the congregation, to be able to do so.

If there is a perceived need for the First Responder Team to provide worship security, the first step is not to visit a gun store or shooting range. The first step should (and must) be to contact an attorney in the area who can guide the Safety Council with regard to the legal requirements for, and limitations on, any form of security team.

The place for worship security

Yes, it seems as though every religious community is forming a security team these days. We know of many shooting instructors and schools that offer training for worship security personnel, and those classes are filling up as the perceived level of violence against religious institutions goes up. It's likely that members of the congregation are no doubt aware of these developments and may push the leadership to form a security team — and in their minds, the sooner the better.

In many cases, dedicated security teams are an over-reaction to the wide publicity given to relatively rare mass-casualty attacks. It's hard to remember, or perhaps even understand, that most risks to the community come not from without, but from within. Good threat intelligence and a security structure that ensures decision makers have the information they need to deal with those threats are the keys to mitigating risk early on, long before worshippers need to start carrying guns.

This isn't to say that worship security is needless or worthless. Many congregations face risks for which a properly trained team is the correct answer. The keys are to understand when formal security is an appropriate tool, and make sure those people properly trained and equipped to perform their duties.

The choice to add security responsibilities to a First Responder Team is a major decision. It should come only after a thorough assessment of the targets, threats, and vulnerabilities the congregation faces.

Duties and limitations

Only after determining the threats and vulnerabilities the congregation faces, and making a thorough assessment of the risks and how best to mitigate them, should the Safety Council consider adding active security duties to a First Responder Team. Without an understanding of what they need to do, it's very easy to overwhelm even the most dedicated volunteers.

. . .

Start by laying out the duties of the team, along with their limitations. What they're not expected or allowed to do may be as important as what they're asked to do.

Define the scope of their security activities based on the risk assessment. Some jobs they may be called on to do include:

- Entry control (greeting)
- Emergency medical response (EMS)
- Keeping the peace
- Responding with force to a lethal attack
- Evacuating worshippers during an emergency
- Notifying 911

They may be asked to provide these services for a wide range of places or activities:

- During regular (scheduled) services
- During special events
- In the office
- At clergy housing

It's easy to see how the tasks assigned to a First Responder Team can quickly exceed the training capacity or number of volunteers. This is why it's essential to clearly define their role and scope of duties before the team is actually formed. In general, giving the team a few well-defined and properly trained tasks, chosen by their importance, is preferable to tasking them with a wide range of duties that strain their training and availability.

Should the First Responder Team be armed?

Before we get into this discussion, it's important to understand where the authors stand on the subject of firearms.

. . .

Both of us are firearms instructors with extensive backgrounds in both armed defense and security. We both teach courses in firearms safety and use on a regular basis, and have many contacts and relationships inside the firearms industry. We are not, by any measure or stretch of the imagination, anti-gun.

At the same time, integrity compels that we discuss firearms in their proper perspective: They are a specialized tool applicable to a very small percentage of security incidents. Our intention is not to talk anyone into, or out of, the idea of an armed First Responder Team. We pledge to give a framework to decide whether armed or unarmed security is appropriate for the community.

As stated at the beginning of the book, armed security is where many congregations start their security planning. The problem is that it's also where too many end their planning. Given the media publicity over mass-casualty attacks, it's often simply assumed that any security team will be armed.

Aside from the legalities, risks are always associated with armed security. These risks make proper oversight a necessity.

Security isn't about shooting bad guys

We hope the preceding chapters have cemented the reality that security isn't always about shooting. Security is about understanding what threats the congregation faces, what targets may be at risk, how vulnerable they are, and only then making plans based on that knowledge.

It's also about ongoing threat intelligence, keeping the Safety Council's figurative eyes open and ears to the ground, and staying on top of evolving issues. Security also includes training the congregation at large how to recognize and deal with potentially dangerous situations, and having plans in place to respond at a moment's notice to an incident.

. . .

Only a small number of those incidents justify the use of lethal force.

Guns are always lethal force

The term "lethal force" may not be familiar, but that's what a firearm represents. Lethal force is the legal term for the use of a firearm, whether it's discharged or not, against another human being. The gun brings with it the possibility of someone dying, which is what makes it lethal.

This requires the user of the gun, and the people who authorize its carry in the house of worship, to come to grips with the fact that someone may die as the result of the use of that gun. It requires an understanding of, and education in, the legal and ethical use of lethal force.

Far too many congregations form armed security teams without understanding this reality or the risks associated with armed security teams.

Risks with an armed team

Wherever there are firearms, there exists a greater-than-zero risk of an accident or a "negative outcome" — an event where the result is worse than the perceived threat. No matter how well trained someone is, there will always be some level of risk involved. This risk needs to be managed, which is another reason any armed security should always have supervision from outside their ranks.

A common issue is the misplaced firearm. Whether armed citizen or law enforcement officer, people have been known to unintentionally leave their guns in places they shouldn't. The restroom is the most common; the armed individual removes their gun to use the toilet, and forgets it when they're finished.

The authors are at a loss to explain why this happens. It seems to us that someone would immediately notice a missing pound-and-a-half of steel and lead on their belt, but for some reason they don't. Not a week goes by that we don't come across yet another report of someone finding a gun in a toilet stall, and very often the find is made by a child. Sadly, the gun is almost always traced back to a licensed gun carrier, law enforcement officer, or federal agent.

Another risk is the unintentional shot, the round fired by accident. In the trade, these are known as negligent discharges or NDs, because they're almost invariably the result of poor gun-handling practices.

Negligent discharges have injured and killed innocent parties, and preventing them is a major focus of most firearms instructors. Still, they can and do happen even with relatively skilled shooters.

If the Safety Council chooses to have an armed First Responder Team, specific protocols for gun handling on-premises will need to be written to prevent misplacements and NDs. There also needs to be enforcement mechanisms to make sure those protocols are followed, and zero-tolerance consequences if they are not.

Again, proper oversight is a necessity — and oversight of an armed team is more difficult than that of an unarmed team. Increased discipline is non-negotiable if armed security is to be an asset rather than a liability.

. . .

Operational dangers

If guns are drawn during an incident, even if the bad guys are subdued, there is always the chance that someone who is not a threat will be injured or even killed. Whether intentional or not, this is a very real risk that must be considered in the decision to have an armed team.

When shots are fired in a confined worship space, the chance of collateral damage is always present. Bullets miss their target, or perforate their target and go on to injure or kill an innocent bystander. While some shooting techniques and ammunition choices can reduce the chance of collateral damage, it is never zero.

It's also possible that, in the heat of a tense incident, someone who is not actually a threat can be intentionally shot. Sometimes it's because of mistaken identity, and sometimes it's because the person with the authorized firearm mistakes an innocent movement for a threatening action and shoots what he believes to be a threat (or another threat).

Finally, there is the possibility of "friendly fire" — the shot that comes from a team member and injures or kills another member of the team. This can happen unintentionally, much as collateral damage does, or it can happen because one team member perceives the presence of another team member's gun as indicative of an attacker.

These are risks any police officer is familiar with. Police officers have gotten shot by other officers, they've shot non-combatants in the honest belief that they saw another threat, and their errant shots have injured innocents.

We point these out not to scare anyone out of having an armed team, but rather to emphasize that armed security is not a zero-risk choice.

Should the congregation choose to have armed security personnel — and we believe the entire congregation should be consulted in the decision — it's essential they receive proper training and frequently practice together as a team.

If the choice is to have armed security, enforced discipline through proper management is an absolute must. It's likely that someone who is not a team member will need to be dedicated to overseeing and enforcing proper training, practice, and procedures to prevent the unthinkable.

Should non-team members be restricted from carrying firearms?

In all states, even those that allow unrestricted carry in a religious structure, the people who own or manage that structure are free to restrict the carrying of firearms. These are private properties, and property owners (or their agents) are almost always allowed to make such decisions.

This is a contentious topic among gun owners. It is our belief that "gun-free zones" do not make people safer. Those who would violate both secular and religious law to murder other people are unlikely to be deterred by a sign saying "No guns allowed."

It is axiomatic, then, that only the law-abiding congregant would obey a prohibition on carrying weapons in a house of worship. We do not therefore believe restricting the lawful carry of firearms will in any way make a congregation safer.

At the same time, many perceive some value in a security-oriented First Responder Team precisely because they know any guns that come out in an emergency likely belong to their team members (whom they know) or an attacker. This, the argument goes, makes identifying the threat in a chaotic situation a little easier. Guns in the hands of congregants they may not know on sight could possibly lead to a tragic mistaken-identity shooting.

While we would like to believe the notion that we can completely control who is armed, the reality is there will always be people who ignore any prohibitions. The security personnel need to understand there may be other guns on the premises, in the hands of people who mean well, and train for the possibility. There is no sure way to prevent mistaken-identity shootings, but being aware of the problem ahead of time will help.

The mixed team

There may be congregants who express interest in being part of a First Responder Team, but don't want to (or for some reason can't) be armed. There's nothing wrong with, and in fact there are some advantages to having a mixed armed/unarmed team.

With an armed team, each member needs to keep constantly aware of where their armed peers are. Knowing who has the guns and where they are is important to preventing friendly fire and mistaken-identity injuries. The fewer armed members, the easier the job of keeping track of each other.

Unarmed team members can perform tasks that armed members would find difficult to do without revealing the presence of their weapons. Greeting people with hugs, for instance, or allowing an elderly congregant to hold on to the waist of someone helping them get around is easier if there's no concern about a concealed firearm getting in the way (or being discovered).

· · ·

Armed team members require far more training, practice, and over-sight, which limits both the number who apply and can be responsibly managed. Having members who don't require that level of investment and oversight makes management easier and enables an expanded team without a corresponding increase in supervisors.

Many times a mixed team results in greater diversity and a better representation of the congregation as a whole. Even in very "conserva-tive" communities, some people don't like firearms and would never consider owning, let alone carrying, a gun. By providing a place for non-armed team members, the First Responder Team may attract people who might not otherwise consider being a part of a "security team".

Having a mixed team has many advantages and very few disadvantages. But there is an important caveat: The unarmed team members must never be treated, or allowed to feel, as though they are in any way lesser than the armed members.

Conversely, the armed members must never be allowed to believe they are somehow better than their unarmed peers (or other congregants). Everyone should focus on the same goal: to protect and serve their fellow congregants so everyone can worship without fear.

Aftermath counseling

In the last few decades, our society has become more cognizant of the need for post-incident counseling. Post-traumatic stress disorder (PTSD) is in fact real, and people who are involved in a violent inci-dent may suffer severe psychological trauma. If someone dies as the result of team's actions, the team members will all be affected.

. . .

This is a very real concern. Many people discount the prevalence of PTSD, or even deny it happens, but we've seen too many people whose lives were destroyed because they were left to work things out on their own after a lethal encounter. If the congregation forms an armed First Responder Team, the congregation is responsible for their well-being — including after an event.

Post-incident or aftermath counseling is, we believe, an imperative. We also believe it needs to be a joint effort of clergy and professional grief counselors. It's vital that the people involved, especially those who actually fired shots, get both religious and medical/psychological support. They need to understand they did the right thing with regard to both the law and the teachings of their faith, and be allowed to work through the very natural guilt and second-guessing they're experiencing.

Clinical depression is an all-too-common result of post-incident stress, and team members should be monitored by a medical professional and given appropriate treatment should symptoms appear.

The rest of the congregation should also be counseled to give their team members proper support. A briefing by a professional can go a long way to helping them say and do appropriate things to help the team recover.

Aftermath counseling is very much a community effort and should be planned before the team is even formed. Waiting until an incident happens, then scrambling to put the necessary response together, is not a responsible way to provide for the team's well-being.

Legal representation for security teams

If an armed team member is involved in a shooting, particularly if there is a fatality, there will be legal fallout. It isn't a matter of "if," but rather "how much."

The team member may be arrested and even face trial. The monetary cost can be huge. If a case goes to trial, the team member can be looking at a six-figure legal bill. Even if the case doesn't go to trial, if the team member has to post bail or retain an attorney for initial representation, they may need to come up with $10,000 (or more) on the spot.

Even unarmed team members can face prosecution for their justifiable actions. If a team member needs to physically restrain someone, any injuries that person suffers are actionable in court. The restraint itself can be construed as kidnapping if it's not performed in accordance with the law — and criminal charges can be pressed.

Can the congregation fund the legal defense of a team member, particularly one who is put on trial? If not, an insurance rider may be needed to cover the legitimate acts of the members of the First Responder Team. If there are any attorneys in the congregation, they should be consulted and asked to consider volunteering as legal representatives should any be needed.

Insurance

Any security team will be a liability to the congregation as a whole. It's important that this liability be understood, accepted, and provided for at the beginning. This includes proper insurance.

The first step is to determine the legal status of a security team in the local jurisdiction. After that's known (and any licensing issues worked out), it's time to consult with the congregation's insurance provider.

Will insurance cover the congregation's liability should a team member cause injury or death? In reality, even if there is no physical injury, the team can be charged with improper detention or impersonation of police. Those are serious charges and the congregation may be financially liable.

What about the team members themselves? A number of companies offer "self-defense insurance" for individuals, but whether they cover a security team member in the performance of their duties is an open question. It's important to have answers to this question and proper guidance provided for both the congregational leadership and the individuals involved.

This is why it's imperative to get input from both legal counsel and insurance professionals before the team is formed. Do not proceed without an understanding of the liabilities involved and policies in place to protect against them.

Preventing "burn out"

Being a member of a First Responder Team, particularly if armed, is a grave responsibility. It's a lot of work to do properly, and keeping up on training and practice can be physically, emotionally, and perhaps even financially stressful.

This doesn't even take into consideration the time team members spend performing their duties for the congregation. Always being "on call" and never being able to sit with their families and enjoy their own worship, are hardships. If they're called to duty for every worship service and routinely for extra services as well, the strain can become too much to bear.

That strain can result in team members leaving and a reduction in membership. The team may even break up if key members quit, leaving the congregation where it started — unprotected.

This means it's important to set a goal of having sufficient security personnel to enable rotating First Responder Teams. One team provides security on a given week so the other team can worship. The next week, the duties rotate to the other team.

This means the Safety Council will need to recruit twice as many security team members as they might think are needed. Keep that in mind as the security planning is being done. Does the congregation have enough interested people? If not, the scope of the First Responder Team's duties may need to be reduced. Adjustments will need to be made in their task list, and complete coverage at all times might not be possible.

Communication systems

Whether armed or unarmed, the First Responder Team needs a method to communicate with each other, to relay important information and call for emergency assistance. Good communications ("comms," as they're known in military and law enforcement circles) are key to maximizing the effectiveness and response of a first responder team.

Being able to talk to each other and to supervisors or decision makers allows a team to dynamically coordinate resources. It puts trained people where they're needed, which gives the team a huge advantage over a threat of any type.

A First Responder Team can communicate in several ways. Most teams use radios, usually on one of the "business band" or General Mobile frequencies[1]. Radios in these frequencies are readily available, rugged, and have a wide range of accessories for covert use. Many teams use these radios with unobtrusive earpieces and microphones in order to be less obvious to the casual observer.

If the team elects to use radios, they'll need to develop shorthand terms for the most common situations they'll encounter, to increase efficiency and reduce airtime. Congregants seeing security personnel engaged in lengthy chats into their microphones may be distracted from worship, and in some cases may actually be alarmed something is happening that they don't know about.

Conflicts with religious tradition

Some denominations have traditions and observances that preclude the carry and use of radios on the Sabbath. In these cases, team members need to develop visual methods of alerting other team members, using abbreviated forms of sign language or audio cues. This means team members need to be in sight or earshot of each other a majority of the time, or rely on a team member whose job is to assume a vantage point where he can see and hear other team members.

Discretion

Discreet is the name of the game in communications. Radio usage should be as unobtrusive as possible so as to minimize both intrusion into worship and to deny onlookers valuable information about security capabilities. The less the average person sees, the better. It's fine that they know some people have radios, but they shouldn't know exactly who has them.

At the same time, it's useful that potential attackers understand comms are in place. What they may have thought was an easy target now appears organized enough to have devices that can summon others. Who are those others? Where are they? How many are there? What else do they have? These are all questions an attacker wants answers to, and not having those answers may be enough to frustrate his plans.

In brief: Be covert until it's time not to be covert. Don't hide comms completely, but don't let anyone see the full extent of the system.

Training the team

The actual training regimen for a security team would require a book of its own, and is therefore beyond the scope of this short chapter. But we can give some general guidelines as to what kind of training the team should have (and what isn't of value).

Specialized "church security training"

Very little in security training is unique to houses of worship. However, in recent years a number of "church security" training courses have sprung up, usually taught by people whose knowledge of security is limited to shooting guns. (In too many cases, they're not terribly qualified to even be teaching that!)

Most of these courses focus on shooting and tend to appear in the aftermath of a highly publicized mass-casualty attack. They prey on the fears of communities that haven't put a comprehensive security plan together and immediately think of lethal force as the answer to their safety concerns.

We hope that by this point in the book, everyone understands that security in houses of worship is far more involved than carrying a gun and knowing how to shoot it. Applied security is mostly about observation, prediction, and pre-emption: knowing what doesn't fit, being able to see emerging issues before they become dangerous, and working to defuse or remove the problem in the least obtrusive manner.

Very little of that involves shooting bad guys. Again, the lawfully carried and used firearm is a tool that's useful only in a small percentage of incidents. "Security training" that focuses almost exclusively on gun handling doesn't help with the majority of incidents where lethal force isn't justified.

If the First Responder Team is going to be armed, it's imperative they get proper training in how to use those firearms, but that's not where their training should start — let alone end.

The ideal skill set

To be truly well-rounded and able to handle all likely contingencies, a First Responder Team should be trained in these areas:

- Verbal de-escalation
- Unarmed (empty hands) defense techniques
- Using contact or impact tools (both for suspect control and defense against non-lethal attacks)
- Recognizing pre-assault indicators
- Spotting concealed weapons

- Advanced first aid (including how to treat massive trauma/blood loss)

The specific facilities or environment may dictate additional skills.

If the First Responder Team is armed, they need specialized shooting skills that focus on rapid threat identification, shooting in crowds, minimizing collateral damage, shooting at extended distances, and safely moving through crowds with guns drawn.

All of their skills need to be trained and then practiced on a regular basis to maintain proficiency. Training isn't the end — it's only the beginning!

Special considerations for the armed team

Aside from the shooting skills detailed above, it's imperative that armed team members have a deep knowledge of the legal and ethical use of lethal force. The gold standard in such training is from the Massad Ayoob Group out of Florida. Their MAG-20 course should be considered mandatory for anyone who is expected to carry a firearm as part of a security team. This course is taught by Massad Ayoob himself all over the United States, in multiple locations every year[2].

(In the interest of full disclosure, the authors are both friends of Massad Ayoob and know many of his staff. However, we have no financial interest in his company and do not benefit in any way from those who take his courses.)

What about recruiting concealed carriers?

The first thought that comes to mind when discussing the idea of armed security teams is simply using congregants who possess concealed carry licenses or permits.

The truth is that concealed carry license training, almost without exception, is completely inadequate for the job of protecting oneself, let alone protecting others. Most license courses are focused on learning the regulations regarding concealed carry, not about using the firearm in an actual defensive shooting.

While some concealed carriers have taken on the self-imposed task of developing excellent defensive shooting skills, they are in the distinct minority. The skills mentioned earlier for armed teams aren't skills that are usually taught in advanced shooting courses, let alone in the basic concealed carry license classes.

Someone with a license to carry may be a good candidate for the additional training necessary to protect the congregation, but they should never be considered properly trained by virtue of their license alone.

Dealing with freelancers

In the world of search-and-rescue, when someone is lost, their friends and family appear at the search site ready to volunteer their services to help find the missing person. While their hearts are in the right place, very often their presence is counter-productive to the search. Their lack of training and knowledge can actually obliterate evidence vital to the search operation.

In many cases they're unprepared for the terrain or conditions, and have been known to get injured and even lost themselves. They end up consuming search and medical resources that can't be used to find or extricate the primary person.

. . .

These well-meaning people are somewhat derisively called "free-lancers," and they're almost always more a hindrance than a help. Well-trained search managers have predefined tasks set aside for them to participate in, tasks that help move the search forward but at the same time don't get in the way of the trained personnel doing the actual work.

Should an incident arise during services, it's almost a guarantee that someone will step in to "help" the First Responder Team. The team needs to be aware of this ahead of time and make contingencies to handle the situation.

The worst scenario is when firearms are involved, because team members may not realize the person holding the gun — and who is not a member of their team — is really a well-meaning good guy. The team needs to take this possibility into consideration during their training and planning.

As we've suggested in the section on risk mitigation, it may be advisable (where legally allowable) to grant congregants permission to carry a concealed firearm on the premises, on the condition that they understand their role as "safeguards of last resort," and that the trained, designated First Responder Team members are the first line of defense and in charge of all incident response. If a First Responder Team member gives them an order or instructions, the armed congregant should be expected to follow it.

What about uniformed security?

Uniformed security, whether in the form of off-duty police officers or a private security service, should never be substituted for an internal security team.

Outside security doesn't know the congregation, its history, membership, or the unique security needs the community faces. They can't perform necessary tasks like greeting and controlling access, as those jobs require an intimate knowledge that only another member has.

What's more, they're unlikely (except at the highest levels) to have the specialized training and knowledge in spotting particular threats that a good security team will. Unless they've been hired and vetted for executive protection expertise, they're unlikely to have any real knowledge of that security specialty.

Private security companies

Private security "officers" undergo only the most cursory training and are almost always poorly paid. As a result, security companies don't get highly skilled or intelligent employees. They are, at best, a form of "window dressing" and serve to deter only the most benign of threats. Sometimes they may not even be successful at that, because there are some individuals who see the uniform as unwelcome authority and may attack because of it, rather than in spite of it.

In most states, training and standards for armed private security are particularly poor. We are very cautious about recommending or using armed private security, because we're intimately familiar with their training and ability. If the congregation must hire private security, they should always be relegated to tasks and positions where being armed is not necessary.

Off-duty police

Police officers working off-duty are certainly more skilled and experienced than any private security firm is likely to be. They typically have a great deal of experience in handling intoxicated and unruly people; if someone is agitated and becoming violent, that experience can be most welcome.

Off-duty officers also have arrest powers and are always qualified to carry firearms. They're extensively trained in the dangerous tasks of subduing and restraining suspects, and they don't run the same legal risks that private security does when placing someone in handcuffs.

They'll also have one very useful tool that the First Responder Team doesn't and can't: a radio that connects directly to dispatch. When they call for help, there will be less of a delay than calling 911, whether they're requesting police, fire, or medical response.

Police officers are not, however, experts in facilities/event security or executive protection. Like private security firms, they're unable to perform tasks that require knowledge of the congregation and religious traditions.

The place for uniformed security

This isn't to say uniformed security has no value. There may in some cases be a deterrent effect from having them on premises, particularly if (as in many jurisdictions) they're police officers using an actual police cruiser. As discussed earlier, however, this doesn't always work.

Uniformed security is best utilized in roles where they're highly visible to the general public and passers-by. Many attacks happen in parking lots, and the presence of uniformed security in those areas may deter the random attacker or uncommitted hothead. They may also deter non-violent crimes, such as vandalism and vehicle break-ins.

The visible deterrent of the uniform must be backed up with the force and authority to respond when someone isn't deterred. It cannot be counted on, by itself, to prevent attacks.

Working with uniformed security

If the choice is made to have uniformed security as part of a total safety strategy, it's imperative that the Safety Council first decide exactly what they are tasked to do. What outcome is expected from their presence? What particular threats are they expected to deter or counter?

Once everyone is clear on what's expected, outline their duties explicitly. It's a mistake (and both of the authors have seen it happen) to hire security and, when they arrive shortly before the event, simply say "protect us." Determine all the details before security is hired: where they'll be stationed, what they're expected to do, and how they'll work with the internal First Responder Team.

It's vitally important that the uniformed personnel meet the First Responder Team ahead of time, and that they understand what their respective roles are. The people in uniform need to be able to recognize the First Responder Team members, identify, and call on them if necessary.

If the First Responder Team uses radios for communication, all uniformed personnel need to be issued one for the duration of their shift. Police radios do not operate on the same frequencies as off-the-shelf radios, so off-duty officers will not be able to communicate with the team if they don't have one of those units.

If both the First Responder Team and the uniformed personnel are armed, being able to identify each other is critical to preventing "friendly fire" incidents. (Again, we strongly recommend armed uniformed security be limited to off-duty police officers.)

This meeting should also include a tour of the facilities, an outline of what to expect during the services, and a detailed discussion of everyone's roles and duties.

Uniformed security should never intrude upon the service or worshippers. Once inside the sanctuary, congregants should feel safe and free to worship as they please. The presence of a uniform, particularly a uniform with a firearm, is detrimental to their experience. For this reason, we recommend that uniformed security be stationed outside the building, or at least in an interior area where they're not intrusive to worshippers.

Special considerations for high-risk clergy

Because clergy often take unpopular moral positions on societal issues, it's not inconceivable that they may be targeted for their activities.

We don't have to look very far for examples. Rev. Martin Luther King Jr. is perhaps the best known, but many other ministers, priests, nuns, and rabbis have also been targeted (and even killed) when certain people took issue with their moral and ethical campaigns.

This is the risk of standing up for anything in today's society. It's conceivable clergy could stand up for a moral position and raise the ire of people outside of the congregation. Some of those people may be violent and put the clergy at risk.

Should that happen, the safety planning may need to involve providing them with the kind of security more commonly associated with VIPs and political figures. This is commonly called "executive protection" and is a specialized form of security.

Executive protection at a glance

The role of these people is to provide close protection for the clergy (or VIP) wherever they go. Some stay with them anytime they are in public. Some even live with the client and rotate shifts so there is an agent guarding them at all times. The actual level of protection is based on the risk level, which is identified by the comprehensive risk assessment steps in earlier chapters.

This is commonly a job that is outsourced to an executive protection firm or a certified executive protection agent hired as an employee to fill the role. In a sufficiently large congregation where enough team members can be recruited, and the budget for the specialized training is available, it might be possible to provide those services "in house". The resources needed are considerable, however, which is why we encourage this job to be outsourced to professionals.

Regardless of whether this expertise is hired or developed, the people doing the job need to be properly trained by a reputable training organization. If specialists are hired for the job, due diligence needs to be done to ensure the protection personnel have been through a recognized course of instruction. If the decision is to task people on the First Responder Team with this job, getting them good training from a specialized executive protection school is critical.

. . .

Schools such as ESI (www.esibodyguardschool.com) and ICON (industry-icon.com) provide excellent training geared toward someone in a high-risk clergy position. They're recognized for their expertise and the quality of their students.

Close protection is very involved and includes tasks that are not obvious to an outside observer. Their activities also need to be integrated with the rest of the safety planning and the First Responder Team, making everyone aware of what the clergy protection team does and how they'll respond to an incident.

Risk assessment for clergy

Any clergy protection team needs to conduct a specialized target-based risk assessment based on the kind of threats public figures commonly face. This assessment should take into account the various environments where they spend time: their home, office, all worship buildings, travel destinations, vehicles, and more.

The decisions about what safeguards should be implemented depend on that risk assessment. This is a skill taught in executive protection courses, which underscores the need for proper training.

If the overall risk assessment (or a developing situation) indicates that higher-level safeguards are needed for clergy, get the right people with the right training in place. Such training can be expensive, but the cost of improper training could be loss of life.

Responsibility

Security tasks can outsourced, but the *responsibility* for security can never be outsourced. In the end, as leaders in the congregation or worship community, the members of the Safety Council are responsible for what the people under their control do. Whether a First Responder Team comes from the membership or is hired from the outside, the responsibility for their actions rests with the Council.

Management can be delegated, but that doesn't relieve the need to supervise. Do not let the First Responder Team(s) operate autonomously. Put into place mechanisms for proper and independent oversight. Have regular reviews, and anytime the team personnel handle an incident, convene a formal meeting and examine what happened. Learn from any mistakes and use them as an opportunity to grow.

Finally, do not hesitate to remove any member(s) of the team should their conduct not meet the previously established standards.

The formation and activation of any First Responder Team, whether armed or not, bring with it a host of issues, liabilities, and responsibilities. It's a lot harder to do properly than it looks.

SELLING THE IDEA TO THE CONGREGATION

The whole subject of worship security is contentious. Many believe that any security planning is an affront to the will of the Creator, while others are intense pragmatists who believe that "God only helps those who help themselves." Of course, a great many (perhaps the majority) hold views somewhere between those extremes.

In order to get necessary security plans put into place (or perhaps even begin the planning process), it will be necessary to elicit support from some segment of the worship community and build from there. Getting that support is often the hardest part of the process. The Safety Council will need to anticipate and answer the likely objections. In short, the congregation has to be sold on the idea.

By popular demand

In some cases, the impetus for greater security comes from the popular opinion of the entire congregation. This is particularly true immediately after a high-profile event such as a school shooting or other mass-casualty attack. People will demand that something be done, which would seem to make the job of selling a security plan easier.

Unfortunately, this is also how bad security plans (particularly those focusing on guns and shooting) get adopted. "Mob rule" often results in superficial, incomplete security. In these instances, the task is not getting people to decide on a security plan, but getting them interested in the *right kind* of security.

In today's society, everyone is looking for the "quick fix." When people are scared, as they are after a highly publicized crime, they're even more inclined to take the easiest path offered[1]. Whether this path actually addresses their needs isn't considered. The risk management approach to security isn't necessarily difficult, but it does require a bit more work and a little extra time. To someone looking for immediate answers, it may not be the attractive option.

At the same time, the risk management path is the best way to establish real security for the community. The conflict between what is expedient and what is best is why others need to be convinced to join the cause. Someone needs to become a cheerleader for safety.

When people need to be convinced

We understand that the notion of selling safety to people is a bit on the crass side. But when dealing with a large group of people — like a congregation — it's a necessary evil. People must be convinced that safety and security is worth the investment of the community's time, money, and energy.

At the start of the safety planning process there will likely be opposition from some members of the congregational community. When the resulting plans start being implemented, there's likely to be still more. The opposition will have reasons why they don't like safety planning, most of them falling into broad groups.

Types of objections

Some of the objections will be financial. In most congregations, money is always an issue. Proper security entails some investment, even if a great deal of the labor is from volunteers. If the security plans underscore the need for a new security system or reinforced doors, for example, the materials must be paid for even if the labor is donated.

Other objections will be practical. Members may feel the new security procedures will impact their own worship or detract from the beauty of the sanctuary. Having security team members greet worshippers at the doors, even in the most benign manner, may be seen as intrusive by some.

If First Responder Team members are armed, that may also be an issue with congregants. Firearms are always a controversial subject, and there will no doubt be those in the community who oppose their presence, regardless of the level of training of the team members who carry them. Knowing a firearm is in the vicinity is enough to scare some people away from worship altogether.

Finally, some people are simply not able to face the realities of our world. They cannot deal with the process of looking at risk and planning ways to mitigate it. They'd rather adopt the "ostrich strategy," putting their minds in the proverbial sand and hoping the bad things just go away. It's often surprising how many of these people there are, and we can almost guarantee that some of them are in every congregation.

. . .

Building consensus

Someone once observed that getting an entire congregation to agree on anything is like herding cats. Everyone wants something different, everyone wants to go their own way, and little hissing fights break out everywhere.

When money is involved, the situation gets worse!

Still, it's necessary to get the congregation's approval in order to put any safety plan into place. In some worship communities, only the approval of the leadership is required to move a project forward, while in others, the congregation as a group needs to be involved.

In either case, getting approval from both the religious and lay leadership is imperative.

Start at the top

For this reason, we suggest starting with the organized leadership of the congregation. They too will have their own preconceptions about what safety planning involves, but dealing with a handful of varied opinions is much easier than dealing with many dozens (or hundreds or, in large congregations, thousands) of differing points of view.

The leadership, to include the clergy, needs to understand the dangers the congregation faces. They must first be educated about the threats and relative risks. If they're already keen to form an armed security team, explain — using concrete examples — that not all threats justify the use of lethal force.

. . .

Emphasize that risk mitigation comes in many forms, from immediate medical response to theft prevention to the "active shooter" scenario. Explain how the security planning and implementation will help protect worshippers from a wide range of threats and keep the house of worship a safe and welcoming place.

Financial projections are a necessary part of this process. Nothing is completely free, and the leadership should know what the security plan will cost the members. Be realistic about the kind and extent of any donations or volunteer contributions.

Finally, explain the shared moral obligation to providing for the safety and security of members, visitors, and clergy. Religious organizations should lead by example, and a comprehensive safety and security plan is an excellent example for others to follow.

Educating the congregation

It's been our observation that this process is, in some ways, easier in large congregations. Many times, large congregations have well-established management and leadership mechanisms, and getting approval (and funding) from that leadership may be enough to put a risk management plan into place.

In smaller congregations, this may not be the case. It may be necessary to appeal to the congregation at large. Our experience suggests that the most vociferous supporters and critics will both be found in the congregation, as opposed to the leadership. The congregation is also where organized opposition may form, driven largely by misconceptions about what security entails.

The task here is to explain the risk management process simply enough for anyone to understand. At the same time, emphasize that there are no quick and easy ways to protect the congregation. We've seen many congregations whose members were under the impression that hiring uniformed security guards was enough to protect their members. In others, allowing people to carry guns under the auspices of a "security ministry" was deemed the best solution.

As we hope we've made clear, neither of those is a comprehensive security solution. Without proper planning and oversight, both of those approaches may be ineffective at best and dangerous at worst.

Not everything should be public

During this education process, it's important that certain specific details of the safety and security plans not be shared with the congregation at large. As discussed in a previous chapter, threats can manifest themselves from within the membership, and it would be best if someone bent on doing harm to others didn't have intimate knowledge of all the security procedures in place.

This is known as operational security, which has the rather ominous acronym OPSEC. The only group that should have full knowledge of the security and response plans for the congregation are the members of the Safety Council, and they should be cautioned about sharing that knowledge with anyone outside of the group.

This means limiting the amount and kind of information shared with the congregation at large. This can make selling the idea to them a bit tricky. They need to have enough information to be able to garner support for the initiative, but not so much detail that the teams can't do their job effectively.

. . .

How much information that's shared, and of what kind, depends on the congregation, the threats it faces, and the plans in place to mitigate those threats. We cannot, however, conceive of a situation where it would be advisable to share everything with everyone.

Navigating treacherous waters

During this process, remember that people's objections are all valid, to them. It's easy to dismiss disagreement, particularly when it comes from people who are very hard to work with (and let's face it, every congregation has members like that!).

The first step, then, is to really listen to and understand their arguments.

Dealing with financial objections

Money, as we've said, is often a very real limitation, and concerns about it shouldn't be brushed aside. If the congregation doesn't have the funds, part of the Safety Council's job will be to find the money necessary to implement the plan.

That might include some sort of fundraising, in the form of quiet appeals to generous members who understand the security issues the worship community faces. It might require looking for savings in the current budget, or implementing the plan over a longer period of time.

It might also include getting people to volunteer to do jobs that would otherwise require paid help. Installing a security system, for instance, might require one knowledgeable person aided by several low-skilled laborers. Volunteers can provide the labor and save the project a not-inconsiderable amount of money.

· · ·

Think through the entire project and present a comprehensive budget (and implementation timeline). Part of that budget should include where the money will come from.

Even with such careful planning and presentation, financial objections will abound. This is where it can be easy — too easy — to resort to fear-mongering to sell the security plan. While some may believe the ends justify the means, we urge everyone to resist this form of coercion.

Instead, focus on the positive benefits of a security plan. Emphasize how it can make worship a more rewarding experience by reducing people's fears, allowing them to devote their thoughts and attention to prayer rather than worrying about who is coming through the doors. Explain how having a First Responder Team not only protects people from attack, but also from mundane (but more common and just as dangerous) medical emergencies.

Not enough people

Especially in smaller congregations, it's easy to quickly outstrip the number or capabilities of available volunteers. Even in larger communities, an overly ambitious plan, covering every activity at multiple locations plus clergy protection, will likely outstrip the potential volunteer pool.

This is a valid argument, and it's a sign that the plan needs to be scaled back to fit the realities of the community's resources. Being a first responder is a daunting task, and not everyone is suited to the necessities of training and commitment. The people who volunteer are going to be a small portion of the congregation. If the First Responder Team members are to be armed, the percentage of people willing to face the possibility of injuring or killing another human being will likely be even smaller.

Answer the manpower argument by carefully planning how the volunteers will be used, and how often any individual will be called on. Use rotating teams to ensure down time for everyone. Don't forget that any security team, armed or not, requires supervision — factor that labor into the plan as well.

Resist the urge to expand the volunteer resources by reducing the training requirements for security teams. As we've discussed, there is a great temptation to look for people with concealed carry licenses and put them on a security team without proper training. Keep the standards high, because the well-being of everyone in the congregation depends on it.

Showing critics that the Safety Council has thought about personnel and have scaled their duties to the realistic pool of available volunteers is the best way to deflect this objection.

Intrusion into worship space

Worship is a highly personal activity. People choose where they worship for a number of reasons, but the ones we hear most often are, "I feel comfortable there" or "It's a welcoming community." Many people worry that a security plan will destroy the reason they belong to the community in the first place.

Any security put into place runs the risk of intruding on the warm, welcoming, comfortable feeling that draws people to the congregation. Everyone has seen pictures or video of the President giving a speech with Secret Service personnel around him. Think of the chilling effect men in suits and dark glasses standing at the back of the sanctuary would have on member's worship.

Worse, think of uniformed police officers doing so, or of uniformed security who use a metal detector on everyone like they were entering a sports arena or courthouse. These are the scenarios everyone thinks of when "security" is mentioned, and it's easy to understand how people might object to that in their house of worship.

Even if this intrusion objection isn't specifically mentioned by opponents, it's always there. It's what we call the "universal objection," because it's always in the back of people's minds. They may use finances or personnel resources as cover for their very real fear of a deterioration in their worship experience.

It may not be actively voiced, but it always needs to be addressed. The best way to handle this fear is to attack it at the start, by emphasizing that safety and security arrangements will always be as low-key as possible under the circumstances. Explain that there won't be people watching them like hawks, or having demeaning interrogations at the door just to get in.

If uniformed security is part of the plan, they should never be allowed inside the sanctuary (and probably shouldn't even be allowed inside the building). The place for uniformed security is outside the building, where they're less a disturbance than a reassuring presence.

Inside the sanctuary, show how the First Responder Team can be essentially unnoticed but still, through judicious placement, communications, and early detection capabilities, be able to respond to any plausible incident.

Part of the intrusion objection relates to architectural or appearance alterations. No one wants to see a beautiful sanctuary defiled by security cameras or sensors. Many houses of worship are historical landmarks in their own right, and modernizations in the form of security systems run the risk of altering the historic nature of their appearance.

Luckily this is the 21st century! Today we have security and surveillance equipment that can be hidden almost anywhere, giving usable coverage without ruining the architectural or decorative elements loved by the community. Explain and show (with manufacturer-provided pictures) how these systems will be installed to be virtually invisible to the congregation, and how little they'll intrude on the ambiance of the worship space.

Other objections

These are the most common objections we've encountered. Humans, being creative entities, are capable of coming up with many more. There are no doubt many objections we haven't covered.

Countering objections is a matter of listening honestly to what people are saying, working to understand them, and accepting that their objections are completely valid — at least to them. Don't belittle or demean any reason for resisting a risk management plan. Worship is a highly personalized experience, and their objections derive from what they may see as an attack on their worship.

Be kind, be empathetic, and work to really understand them. Then explain in terms important to them that the proposed security won't affect them adversely. In some cases, the objections will be well-founded; be ready to adjust the plan to address them.

Rest assured that if one person feels security is an affront to their worship experience, many others do too, but simply don't have the courage to speak up. By listening to all objections honestly and addressing them respectfully and thoughtfully, more than just one person will be reached.

Be honest, be realistic

It's tempting to try to be all things to all people, to answer all objections with firm promises. Don't fall into that trap. Understand there are some objections that can't be overcome, and that not all concerns or fears can be answered.

At the same time, the leadership and/or the congregation's expectations need to be realistic. There is no "silver bullet" in security, and those who expect absolute guarantees will never be happy — that is, if the process and the people doing it are honest and transparent.

Sometimes such irrational expectations may, in fact, doom the risk management process to failure. If someone or some group won't be reasonable and logical about the process and the end results, leaving the congregation unprotected, members of the Safety Council may themselves have a hard decision to make: Is the reward of belonging to that worship community worth the unmitigated risks?

DEALING WITH THE AFTERMATH

Part of any safety plan needs to be consideration for what happens after an incident. It doesn't matter the size or nature of the incident; every single one has an impact on the security plan, the response, the responders, and the congregation. This is especially true when the incident involves a death or serious injury.

In the not-too-distant past, first responders such as law enforcement, firefighters, and emergency medical personnel were left to their own devices after a traumatic experience. Today we recognize that doing so is not only irresponsible, but also damaging to their emotional and psychological health.

Victims also experience significant issues when they're left to deal with an incident on their own. Personal, professional, and family relationships can suffer if unresolved feelings and beliefs are allowed to percolate through their conscious and subconscious minds.

. . .

From the standpoint of the safety and response plans, every incident is a learning experience. First Responder Teams can learn what does and doesn't work and hone their actions accordingly. A properly implemented review process can help them become better at their task, to keep the people who rely on them safe and sound during the next incident.

Comforting the victims

People who are impacted by an incident always go through a recovery process. Even a relatively minor incident, one that most people forget about in a matter of hours after it happens, can for others serve as a trigger that causes them to remember a previous and much more traumatic event.

Religious communities tend to be very good at comforting people. It's part of many faiths and is an area of specialty for some. Helping people who are going through rough times is part and parcel of the doctrine for many denominations.

After an incident, this comfort will be sorely needed. Part of the response plan should be an organized outreach to the victims, plus the congregation as a whole should be reminded to reach out, informally, to their fellow members who are having a difficult time processing their thoughts and feelings.

Enlist the aid of counseling professionals who may be members of the community. Psychological counseling may be as important as faith counseling, so make those resources available to people who need them.

The designated healers may themselves need help too. If they've been victims, they may need counseling to be able to process their own issues and help others through the process. This is especially true after a death, as grief can be difficult for anyone to move through.

Don't be afraid to reach out to others, even outside professionals, for this help. The religious community may be good at counseling, but until the healers are able to recover, they'll need someone else helping them to help others.

Also, don't neglect the possibility that those community members who are normally the "rocks" whom everyone can lean on may be the ones having the toughest time recovering from an incident. Identify those key members and make sure they have the resources they need for their own recovery.

The youngest members of the community may need the most help. Part of growing up is learning to deal with adversity, but those who haven't yet become adults won't know how. They will not fully understand the incident as they saw it, and as their minds grapple with processing those memories, thoughts may emerge that could haunt them for many years.

Getting children of all ages the professional help they need, early on, is something we should not hesitate to do.

Don't forget those who are in charge of the children, from sitters to religious school teachers. They need to be protected not just physically, but also emotionally and spiritually. They'll need help to move through their own recovery, and to help the children in their care to cope with their thoughts and feelings as well.

· · ·

As a community, people's role in the recovery process is just as important as in the response preparation. Those in charge of the safety and security planning must have the foresight to put safeguards in place that help with the recovery after an incident.

There is a bright side: These are the times when we generally see the good people of the world come out. Embrace those kind and courageous people, and let them help.

Reassuring first responders

In the past, the people on the front lines — the first responders — were completely ignored in what little recovery process there was. Grant's father was a first responder in the small town where he grew up; his father saw friends and neighbors suffer grievous injuries and even deaths, and at that time there was no such thing as counseling. The firefighters and ambulance crews were left to their own devices to cope with their experiences, and some were more successful than others. Those who weren't often suffered long-term effects that changed their lives for the worse, and sometimes their internal demons won the battle.

Today our police, firefighters, and EMS personnel can avail themselves of counseling professionals who help them put the horrors they see on a daily basis into proper perspective. The congregation's first responders deserve no less.

After any incident where injury or death is involved, regardless of exactly who is hurt, the First Responder Team should get some down time. Counseling resources, both religious and medical, should be made available, and the team should understand these resources are there for them.

. . .

When death is involved

If casualties come at the hands of the security responders, even when the suspect was the only one hurt or killed, those involved will need special attention. They need to understand their actions were just, that they did the right things for the right reasons.

Death is always a particularly hard thing to process. Religion teaches peace and understanding, and any death seems contrary to deeply held principles. But all the religions we're familiar with allow, and in some cases require, defense in the face of death. Even the most pacifistic denominations we've encountered make allowances in their doctrine for defense of self and others.

The defender who causes the death of another person, even when that other person was a clear and immediate threat to the lives of others, often feels ostracized by their friends, neighbors, and even families. Well-known use-of-force expert Massad Ayoob calls this the "Mark of Cain Syndrome." The defenders need reassurance from their faith community that their actions were just and the community appreciates their actions in keeping them safe and will support them through the recovery process.

Watch the "tough guys"

Response and security operations tend to attract "Type A" personalities, the hard-charging people who are able to act when others recoil. Those positive traits become liabilities in the recovery process, as many of those tough personalities will arrogantly insist they're strong and don't need anything as demeaning as counseling.

Many times these are the people who need counseling the most, as they hide their inability to process their feelings behind a strong veneer. Make sure they're aware that counseling is private and confidential, and that no one need know they received it. In some extreme cases, the leadership may have to insist that overly defiant members be suspended from duty until they've spoken with a professional counselor.

Reviewing the response

Every incident, no matter how small, should be formally reviewed. As we discussed earlier, After-Action Reviews (AARs) should be done for every incident — after ample time for recovery has occurred, but not so long after that memories have faded.

A major incident may need a month of recovery and preparation for the AAR, while a minor one might be covered the week after. In no case should the AAR be done more than three months afterward. This keeps the event fresh in the mind but also allows the all-important recovery period after the event.

How to start the AAR

Every person involved in the incident is likely to have a different perspective of how things occurred. Some details will be foggy, and not everyone will be able to recall exactly what they themselves did — let alone others.

One of the ways to get a clear picture is to walk everyone through a narrative of the incident. If there is a police report, use that as the guide. Ask questions about what people were doing or thinking at particular specific points. Start with those people, both responders and the community at large, who were in the immediate area and had the best view of the situation. Ask them to insert their thoughts at particular parts of the narrative where they were involved or actively observing the scene.

Memories are fragile

One pitfall to watch for are those people who try to "drive" others' recollections based on their own perspective or belief about how the incident unfolded. Many times their forceful opinions lead others to modify their own testimony in order to go along with them. If everyone is to get a clear picture and make better plans for the future, the facilitator of the AAR has to be able to recognize when this is happening and control the process to prevent it.

In the last decade, science has shown us that memories, particularly of traumatic incidents, are not recalled so much as reconstructed — based on the knowledge and biases of the person involved. Because of this, it's easy to implant memories of things that didn't really happen, or happened differently. An overly strong personality who is convinced of their own infallibility can cause others to reconstruct their memories differently than they might have otherwise. Once reconstructed, it can be difficult or impossible to get objective viewpoints on what actually happened.

Be careful that certain forceful people do not drive other's thinking on how the incident occurred, based on their own (often flawed) perspective.

Learn from the experience

Once everyone has participated in the review with a sufficient amount of factual detail, it's time to talk about what could have been done better or differently.

. . .

Start with the people who were closest to the incident — first the responders themselves, then close observers. Work outward in proximity to others who were outside of the immediate area. Listen to their ideas of what went right, what didn't go so right, and if applicable, where things went badly wrong. From all of those viewpoints will emerge ideas on how to change procedures and priorities to prevent similar things from happening in the future.

If possible and appropriate, it might be valuable to bring in an outside party to give their opinions on what the first responders did. If there was a police or EMS response, for instance, their perspective may be very important.

The goal of the AAR is to get a lot of feedback in order to make a list of things that went wrong or could have been done better. That list is used to make (or amend) a mitigation plan to address the specific issues.

Document everything

It's important that this whole process be thoroughly documented. This is for both practical and legal reasons.

Having a document that can be reviewed at a later date may help guide the mitigation planning, serve as a training aid, and allow future perspectives on the incident. It may also help if insurance coverage is needed, as well as serving as legal proof that any deficiencies were addressed.

If a team member is relieved of duty for misconduct, the documentation of exactly what happened may help in any lawsuit that might be brought by the aggrieved member.

. . .

At the very least, a comprehensive written record of the proceedings is needed, though audio/video recordings may be advisable as well.

Dealing with the media

In dealing with the media, not every interaction will be for the good.

Depending on the kind of incident, the bias of the reporter and their organization, and the general mood of the community, coverage of an incident in the congregation may range from strongly sympathetic to downright hostile. The worst part is that it might not be obvious which until it's too late.

We recommend that, whenever possible, professional public information officers from police or fire services handle media inquiries. They have the training and experience to handle the sometimes duplicitous nature of the news cycle and likely will personally know the reporter(s) involved.

Some clergy training includes dealing with the media. If the religious leadership has had that training, they should serve as the media point of contact. If not, they should refer reporters to someone who has.

Many organizations that deal with disaster planning have short courses in media relations, with the aim of making attendees official public information officers for their agencies. These courses are offered through state and regional emergency management agencies, search-and-rescue organizations, and disaster responders such as the American Red Cross and amateur radio emergency services. If possible, have at least one First Responder Team member attend such training and task them with the job.

If there are no trained or professional media resources available, we suggest avoiding all but the most superficial comments. Assume the media is not friendly to the community or cause. Don't give out any details or names connected with the incident, but rather focus on how the community is praying for healing for all involved. Refer any further questions to the community's legal representatives.

Rebuilding the faith community

After any major incident, there will be a wide range of responses inside the congregation. Some may be wholly supportive of the response, others vocally critical, and still others somewhere in the middle.

This divergence of opinion carries the risk of fracturing the bonds of the worship community. The more dangerous the incident, the more damage to the community. An incident involving death (particularly multiple deaths) or significant property damage may split the community irreparably.

It's important that the spiritual rebuilding process start immediately. The people have to be brought together, differences addressed and arguments settled, so the community stays whole.

This is where the religious leadership is most needed. It will be their job to hold the community together, smooth over anger and resentment, and help people focus on what is important. Rebuilding the community should be a specific section in the recovery plan, and clergy should understand they are central to the process.

PUTTING IT ALL TOGETHER

We are keenly aware that everyone wants a shortcut, particularly when dealing with complex or difficult issues such as community security. It's tempting to look for a "one size fits all checklist" and be able to say, "Yes, we've planned for security."

The problem is that every congregation is different. There isn't, and can't be, a checklist that works for every community when it comes to putting together a risk mitigation plan for places of worship.

But it is possible to lay out the process in a way that makes it easy to follow and implement. With that in mind, this chapter outlines a generalized illustration of the process in creating such a plan. It's intended as a sort of "Cliff's Notes" guide to the rest of the material we've presented, to help see the whole process in one place.

Every process is different

When creating a customized plan for use in any given place of worship, the exact process might out of necessity look slightly different than what we show. That's perfectly fine!

What follows is an outline of the possible things that might be included in the process, but it is by no means a definitive plan. Feel free to modify this guide as necessary to meet the specific needs of the congregation. If, for example, the congregation has already accepted the idea of having a First Responder Team provide security, there is no need to "sell" the leadership on the concept. That step can be ignored.

If something doesn't fit the needs of the congregation, skip past it. It's easy to get bogged down in process overhead, particularly in small congregations, and end up not getting anything important done. Use what's needed, but don't try to shortcut the process.

Human resources

This is especially true in terms of team membership. Ideally there would be a separate group or committee to handle every function we've listed, but that isn't always (or probably ever) possible. Consider not only the overall size of the congregation, but also the size of the much smaller pool of interested people. It's not unusual to have the same people handling all the roles.

That's perfectly acceptable, except for one role: that of supervising the First Responder Team. Supervision needs to be separate from the membership of the team; the person or people taking on the supervisory role should never be members of the First Responder Team themselves.

This oversight includes making sure the members are following protocol and not taking advantage of, or liberties with, their authority.

It should be obvious that this oversight cannot be done by someone who is personally invested in the outcome. It's difficult, if not impossible, for a team member to objectively assess the actions of the others on the team — let alone themselves.

Ideally, that supervision will come from the Safety Council itself, though it may be useful to form a separate committee for the express purpose of First Responder Team oversight.

The important point is that the team not be allowed to manage itself, particularly if the choice of armed security is made.

Repetition is important

Keep in mind that security planning and implementation are repeating cycles. Just because all the items have been addressed once doesn't mean the job is complete! The plan needs to be set up in such a way that regular reviews and revisions happen as the environment around the congregation changes.

It's also important to work out a maintenance routine for the risk management process itself, so that assessments are continually re-examined. If that doesn't happen, over time even the most comprehensive plan can become obsolete and therefore ineffective.

Step 1: Organizing people

This step is where the basics of security, including first responder groups, organized teams to do specific tasks, and the Target-Based Risk Management method, are introduced. For some congregations, this may include the need to sell the very notion of increasing security and safety for the benefit of everyone.

. . .

Most of these steps are likely to be needed:

- Recruit and organize the Steering Group: These are the people who will do the oversight of the planning and implementation, serve as liaison to the congregational leadership, and establish and maintain budgets. They may also serve as oversight to the operational security teams. The Steering Group forms the core of the Safety Council.
- Sell the first responder concept: Convince the congregational leadership that security planning is important and a moral obligation.
- Recruit and organize the Planning Group: These are the people who will do the bulk of the planning work. They do the assessments, set up and perform the plan audits, put together proposals for specific mitigation activities, and make implementation plans. In smaller congregations, there may be no separate group; these activities are handled by everyone on the Safety Council.
- Document restrictions: Establish the limits of scope and authority at the very beginning. This includes what the Safety Council *won't* be doing. These limits are vital to keeping the process on track.
- Recruit and organize First Responder Team(s): These are the people who will do the actual day-to-day work of keeping the congregation safe. First responder duties may include security (armed or unarmed), medical/trauma care, facilities security, clergy protection, entry/access monitoring, and security-system monitoring.

Step 2: Risk analysis

The second major step in the process is conducting a risk analysis. This is where the real, versus the perceived, threats to the place of worship and congregation are identified along with their impact on the broader community. This is the critical part of the entire safety and security process; without this information, budgeting, resources, and risk mitigation plans can't be made.

Without risk analysis, no one will know who or what will be protected, what they're being protected from, or how to do it effectively. Implementing any kind of security without a risk analysis is foolhardy and likely to be a waste of valuable resources. This step cannot be skipped!

This step is usually done by the Planning Group, if it exists.

- Target assessment: Identify those things that are at risk. This includes people, facilities, finances, and information.
- Threat assessment: List the active and proximate dangers that might damage or destroy a target. Threats pose the possibility of death or loss; they are the things we're protecting against/from.
- Vulnerability assessment: Determine the features and activities where targets are susceptible to being wounded, damaged, or destroyed. Vulnerabilities are the intersection of targets and threats, and include collateral damage.
- Environmental assessment: Establish any variances based on the environments (place, time, activity) each target occupies.
- Incident assessment: Identify the kinds of events, both intentional and unintentional, that could result in some kind of loss. These are correlated with threats, targets, and vulnerabilities to determine the risk.
- Risk assessment: Based on the targets, threats, vulnerabilities, and likely incidents, produce a weighted score to indicate the importance or priority for protection and allocation of mitigation resources.

Step 3: Risk mitigation

The third step in the process is risk mitigation. In this step, we create the strategy for reducing the impact of the high-risk incidents that were identified in Step 2. Part of this step is to work with the congregational leadership to allocate resources for risk reduction projects.

If it exists, the Planning Group leads this process, working closely with the rest of the Safety Council (Steering Group and First Responder Team) to put the identified safeguards in place.

- Select a mitigation strategy: For each identified risk, choose to Reduce, Transfer, Avoid, or Accept the risk.
- Decide on safeguards: For each risk, decide on an appropriate safeguard that minimizes the risk's impact on the target. For example, if it's decided to transfer risk, identify specifically how that's to be done (insurance policy, etc.)
- Present the safeguards to leadership: Give the congregational leadership (or others as appropriate) the list of the risks and the safeguards that best to mitigate that risk.
- Prepare and present budget: Determine how much each mitigation choice is going to cost, both in terms of money and labor (volunteer involvement). For any purchases, get more than one estimate.
- Implement safeguards: Once approved, put those safeguards in place and make them operational.

Step 4: Training, testing, & documentation

This is where most congregations mistakenly start. Without knowing the risks the worship community faces, it's impossible to know what to train for! This step can come only after the preceding steps have been addressed to some degree.

. . .

Don't neglect the documentation parts of this process. In order to do a conscientious and defensible job, the Safety Council must be able to show what they did, why they did it, when it happened, and who was involved.

- Create incident policies and procedures: This is part of the policy and procedure manual that outlines the response plans to high-risk incidents. The Planning Group would ideally work closely with the First Responder Team(s) to create the manual.
- Test incident procedures: Plans are tested through role-playing scenarios, tabletop, or other exercises that allow everyone involved to clearly visualize the processes and look for issues.
- Document response plan issues: Make sure that every possible issue is clearly identified and propose solutions. Any personnel or equipment deficiencies should be listed.
- Fill gaps in response skills/equipment/procedures: This may involve purchasing, recruiting, or amending the response plans to better utilize resources. Some gaps may be caused by lack of training. If so, seek out training to fill those specific gaps.
- Conduct training exercises: All first responders should be thoroughly and properly trained, and that training should be practiced at regular, scheduled intervals. Training exercises may also involve clergy and, in some cases, the congregation at large.

Step 5: Plan maintenance & auditing

The final step in the process is maintenance and auditing of the plans. This is a recurring step that should be scheduled periodically (or as ongoing threat intelligence dictates changes be made). Auditing the safeguards periodically ensures they're still functioning as intended. Complacency, or lack of auditing, can cause safeguards to become ineffective.

. . .

This step also includes the need for periodic training to ensure responders' skills are fresh and up to date, so they can provide quick and efficient response to the incidents they've prepared for.

- Re-evaluate risks: Go back through the risk assessments and determine if they're still valid. Some may increase, others decrease, and some disappear altogether.
- Update documentation: Make sure all of the threat intelligence, training, auditing, and operational manuals are up to date and valid.
- Audit safeguards and incident procedures: Determine the current applicability and usability of all equipment and response procedures. Make sure first-aid kits are within expiration, batteries changed/charged, etc.
- Evaluate skillsets: Test first responders to ensure they can perform their skills safely, efficiently, and effectively.
- Continual training: Retrain the first responders any time a safeguard, procedure, or policy is updated. Ensure responders hold regular practices and receive additional or continuing education in their area(s) of specialization, and that appropriate members are suitably cross-trained.

CLOSING THOUGHTS

Just as we were putting the finishing touches on this book, a horrific attack on a synagogue in Pittsburgh, PA happened. In the middle of their prayers, eleven people were killed by a lone gunman whose hate for the people in that sanctuary led him to scream "All Jews must die!" as he opened fire.

Almost immediately, there were calls all over the country for houses of worship (particularly synagogues) to arm themselves. Several shooting instructors hopped onto the publicity train by offering free shooting classes for synagogue members.

Absent in all the posturing and fear-mongering was any discussion about comprehensive approaches to congregational security. Without that, most houses of worship will remain — like the one in Pittsburgh — soft targets.

What we've presented in this book is a comprehensive yet understandable approach to the problem of safety and security planning. Target-Based Risk Management is the professional approach to the problem, and it was our goal to make this sometimes arcane specialty usable by ordinary people. We hope we've succeeded!

As we said at the beginning, there is a collective moral obligation to see to the safety and well-being of everyone who gathers under the auspices of any congregation, worship community, sect, denomination, or religious tradition. But doing so effectively can only happen through a thoughtful, organized approach to the problems.

Don't wait for disaster to visit your congregation. Get started today.

We have a favor to ask...

If you found this book useful, we'd appreciate your review on either Amazon or the Apple iBooks store!

Amazon review link: www.getgrant.us/ps-kindle

iBooks Store review link: www.getgrant.us/ps-apple

APPENDIX: CARVER+S+P CRITERIA SCALES

Risk assessment is, by its nature, a somewhat subjective activity. But by using scales of magnitude, we can bring some objectivity into the rankings. Here are some suggested scales for use with the CARVER+S+P method introduced in the Risk Assessment chapter.

C: Criticality

How would an attack damage the ability of the target to serve its purpose or fulfill its objectives? We measure criticality in terms of the amount of damage — in lives and value — that a threat could cause.

Scale: Measurable effect

9-10: Loss of over 50 lives, over 100 injured, OR loss of more than $1 million

7-8: Loss of 25 – 100 lives, over 50 injured OR loss of $250,000 to $1 million

5-6: Loss of 5 – 25 lives, over 25 injured, OR loss of $100,000 - $250,000

3-4: Loss of 1-5 lives, over 5 injured, OR loss up to $100,000

1-2: No likely loss of life, insignificant injuries or monetary loss

A: Accessibility

Accessibility is the openness of the target to the general public. It measures the ease with which the threat can actually reach the target, or how impeded it is. For intentional threats, accessibility also includes how easy it is for the threat to get information (intelligence) that makes an attack possible. In those types of attacks where the threat expects to get away with the crime, it also includes how easily the threat can get away without notice or apprehension.

Scale: Ease of access

9-10: Easily accessible; little to no impediments in place. Target surveillance or planning probably not needed; most at risk for random attacks. No disaster prevention in place.

7-8: Somewhat accessible; impediments easily bypassed with little knowledge or skill. No tools or equipment likely to be needed, though surveillance may be. Disaster mitigation and training minimal.

5-6: Partially accessible; noticeable impediments requiring knowledge, skill and/or tools to bypass. Surveillance and preplanning very important to success of the attack. Disaster mitigation present but doesn't address all hazards.

3-4: Hardly accessible; significant impediments require knowledge, skill, and/or tools to defeat. Surveillance and preplanning critical to success. Disaster preparation and training extensive and regularly audited.

1-2: Not accessible. Highly protected from surveillance, attack, and disaster. Successful attack would require multiple participants, weapons, extensive preplanning and insider knowledge of the target.

The first R: Recuperability

How long would it take the target to recover full operation or to continue its mission if faced with significant damage or destruction?

Scale: Timeline of recovery

9-10: Greater than 1 year recovery time, insurance insufficient and significant outside-of- community fundraising required. Significant contribution of volunteer labor necessary to augment outside contractors.

7-8: Recovery 6 months to 1 year; insurance may not cover everything, requiring the congregation to raise the remaining portions necessary. Outside contractors and expertise required. Volunteer labor plays a large role.

5-6: 3-6 month recovery. Insurance likely to cover all costs; outside contractors likely necessary, though the majority of the labor is likely to come from volunteers aided when necessary by hired craftspeople.

3-4: 1 to 3 month recovery time. All labor and expertise found inside the community, though outside contractors may be desired to speed the recovery process.

1-2: Less than 1 month recovery. Funds available from operational budget, very little to no need for an insurance claim. No particular expertise needed, labor easily provided by volunteers from within the congregation.

V: Vulnerability

How easy is it to damage or destroy the target? Vulnerability specifically ranks weaknesses in the target that the threat can exploit. Some of the factors are the same as those for accessibility, but vulnerability focuses on the harm that can be caused as a result of gaining access.

Scale: Characteristics of the target

9-10: Target very vulnerable; access and damage resistance combine to make damage inevitable, even with interdiction.

7-8: Conditions almost always allow access of sufficient force or other agents to make target damage very likely; interdiction may not always be effective or possible

5-6: Better than even probability that target can be damaged or destroyed by threat; interdiction often but not always effective.

3-4: Only moderate likelihood that the threat can apply enough resources to cause the desired damage. Interdiction often very successful.

1-2: Very low probability that the threat can apply enough resources to do any damage. Interdiction highly successful, passive protection often sufficient.

E: Effect

This measures the amount of disruption a threat could have on the normal, every day functions of the congregation. This includes the time of clergy, volunteers, as well as time the facilities are open to members and non-members. It may also include political, economic, legal, and psychological effects.

Scale: Amount of disruption

9-10: Crippling disruption; greater than 50% of the congregation's activities affected or curtailed.

7-8: Significant disruption; 25-50% of the congregation's activities are affected

5-6: Minor disruption; 10-25% of the congregation's activities are affected

3-4: Minimal disruption; 5-10% of the congregation's activities are affected

1-2: Less than 5% of the congregation's activities are affected; essentially no disruption.

The second R: Recognizability

How easy is it for the attacker to recognize the target? How much intelligence is needed for recognition? When talking about buildings, this is easy because they don't change and don't move. But for a human target, recognizability can be significantly affected by many factors. This includes ease of intelligence gathering; if it's easy to get the information the threat needs, the recognizability is higher.

Scale: Ease of recognition

9-10: Target is clearly recognizable, requiring little or no training or reconnaissance to clearly identify. Buildings with large, clear signage and all-condition lighting fall into this category.

7-8: Target is easily recognizable, requires only minimal training/surveillance for recognition.

5-6: Target is difficult to recognize or easily confused with another target; requires some training or surveillance for positive recognition. Nondescript buildings often fall into this category.

3-4: Target is difficult to recognize; easily confused with other targets and requires extensive surveillance and reconnaissance for recognition.

1-2: Target cannot be recognized under any conditions, except by experts backed by a wide amount of information gleaned from intelligence and reconnaissance operations. Very few, if any, civilian targets fit into this category.

+S: Shock addition

This addition accounts for the psychological, sociological, and historical losses that don't have intrinsic value but are important to the congregation and the surrounding community. While shock is increased with human or economic losses (see the criticality measurement), those aren't required for a target's destruction or damage to have significant psychological shock.

Scale: Effect on population

9-10: Target has national-treasure-level historical, cultural, religious, or other symbolic importance. Major impact on sensitive subpopulations, e.g., children or elderly, outside of the incident community. May include major loss of life and national economic effects. International news event. Presidential level attention almost certain.

7-8: Target has high historical, cultural, religious, or symbolic importance, perhaps extending regionally. Impact on sensitive subpopulations is significant, extending beyond the incident zone itself. High loss of life and state-level economic effects may be included. National media present, may also receive limited international attention. May receive federal-level political attention; state-level attention is certain.

5-6: The target is considered to have moderate historical, cultural, religious, or symbolic importance, primarily in the immediate local area. Impact to sensitive subpopulations limited largely to the incident area, but can extend beyond the local area. May include significant loss of life or local economic effects. Media attention will be regional and may attract limited national media; state-level political involvement likely.

3-4: Target has little historical, cultural, religious, or symbolic importance. Impact to sensitive subpopulations is small, limited largely to direct victims. Little loss of life or economic impact likely.

Media attention is likely to be local and superficial; political involvement may not extend beyond the municipality.

1-2: Target has no real importance other than to the congregants. No impact on subpopulations, no loss of life and little economic impact. Will not attract political attention beyond the local neighborhood, and media is unlikely to recognize the event occurred.

+PoW: Place of Worship addition

This is our addition to the assessment criteria, focusing on the worship community's reluctance to enact changes to their safety/security posture. Strong resistance results in an increase in the congregation's susceptibility to damage from identified threats, and needs to be accounted for when determining overall risk. It may vary depending on the type of safeguard being proposed.

Scale: Resistance of the congregation

9-10: Strong pacifist, religiously traditional, or fiscally conservative views throughout members and leadership. Makes prevention, mitigation, or response functions exceptionally difficult to implement.

7-8: Approximately 3/4 of the members and leaders exhibit opinions or traits that make it very difficult to put comprehensive safety/security plans into place.

5-6: Roughly half of the members and leaders display those opinions or tendencies. Somewhat difficult to find sufficient support to put plans together and implement them.

3-4: Less than 1/4 of the members and/or leadership have moral, religious or fiscal objections to safety/security plans. Minimal resistance to prevention, mitigation, or response functions.

1-2: Most of the congregation and leadership are either supportive of, or are neutral with regards to, safety and security planning. Large contingent of strong support makes it relatively easy to fund and staff the necessary planning and implementation.

CHAPTER FOOTNOTES

WHY RELIGIOUS SPACES ARE HARD TO SECURE

1. If you want to dive deeply into these topics from a Christian point of view, Greg Hopkins has an outstanding book titled *A Time to Kill* that covers all the arguments exhaustively. Another excellent book that examines the topic from both Christian and Jewish perspectives is *The Morality of Self-Defense and Military Action: The Judeo-Christian Tradition* by David B. Kopel.

THREAT ASSESSMENT

1. *Such an event occurred in Quebec in 2013, when a train derailment, explosion, and resulting fires destroyed more than 30 buildings and killed 47 people in the small town of Lac-Mégantic. Nearby rail lines and highways should always be considered threats.*
2. *https://blog.nssl.noaa.gov/nsslnews/2009/03/us-annual-tornado-death-tolls-1875-present/*
3. *King, Wayne. "Blast Kills 21 Outside Church in Alexandria, Egypt." www.reuters.com/article/us-egypt-church-blast-idUSTRE6BU2VR20110101*
4. *Gadahn, Adam. "A Call to Arms" [Video, 2010] and "Convert or Die" [Video, 2006]*
5. *www.dhs.gov/state-and-major-urban-area-fusion-centers*
6. *https://www.officer.com/home/article/10249289/inside-an-arsonists-mind*
7. *Johnson, Stephen: Humanizing the Narcissistic Style; and Character Styles. Both W. W. Norton & Company. (1994)*
8. *https://www.rainn.org/about-sexual-assault*
9. *https://www.childmolestationprevention.org/pdfs/study.pdf*
10. *www.rainn.org/statistics/criminal-justice-system*
11. *Department of Justice, Office of Justice Programs, Bureau of Justice Statistics, National Crime Victimization Survey, 2010-2014 (2015). www.bjs.gov/index.cfm?ty=pbdetail&iid=5366, and Department of Justice, Office of Justice Programs, Bureau of Justice Statistics, Sexual Assault of Young Children as Reported to Law Enforcement (2000).*

VULNERABILITY & RISK ASSESSMENT

1. *www.fema.gov/media-library/assets/documents/2150*
2. *We are using the masculine out of convenience, not to imply that all clergy are male.*

WHAT ABOUT WORSHIP SECURITY TEAMS?

1. *www.fcc.gov/wireless/bureau-divisions/mobility-division/industrial-business*
2. *www.massadayoobgroup.com/mag-20-classroom/*

SELLING THE IDEA TO THE CONGREGATION

1. *We say this with the utmost of caution: It's easier for people to grasp the urgent nature of risk management in the immediate aftermath of a horrific incident, no matter where that incident occurred. We are not suggesting you wait for something bad to occur, nor are we in any manner condoning the "dancing in the victims' blood" that always results from any attack. We simply point out the sad fact that urgency is more keenly felt when something is fresh in one's mind. Using recent incidents as learning opportunities may be one way to get your message across.*

FACEBOOK DISCUSSION GROUP

We've put together a private Facebook group just for readers of Praying Safe!

It's a moderated, restricted discussion group where you can communicate with others who share your concern for protecting places of worship. Talk about your problems, successes, concerns, and get tips from the authors to better implement the target-based risk management approach in this book.

The group will also get advance notice of workshops and new editions of the book!

Just go to:

https://www.facebook.com/groups/prayingsafebook/

...and click the "Join" button!

COMING SOON: THE PRAYING SAFE WORKBOOK

There's a lot of detail work in the job of securing a worship community. Doing the right things, in the right order, and keeping track of it all can be a big job.

Our companion workbook will make that job easier! The **Praying Safe Workbook** combines blank forms, checklists, and step-by-step guides to doing all of the assessments and planning we talk about in **Praying Safe: The professional approach to protecting faith communities**.

The **Praying Safe Workbook** will be released in the first months of 2019, but you can get advance notice of the release by signing up to the mailing list!

Just go to this link:

www.getgrant.us/PSW

...and you'll be able to sign up for the mailing list and receive advance notification when the Workbook is available for purchase. In addition, we'll be sending complimentary pre-release copies to random members of the mailing list for their feedback. You may be the lucky one who gets a free copy!

(Don't worry, we'll treat your email address as confidential; it will not be sold to or shared with anyone else.)

OTHER TITLES BY GRANT CUNNINGHAM

Protecting Your Homestead: *Using a rifle to defend life on your property*

Prepping For Life: *The balanced approach to personal security and family safety*

Protect Yourself With Your Snubnose Revolver

How To Choose Defensive Ammunition

Handgun Training: *Practice Drills For Defensive Shooting*

Defensive Revolver Fundamentals

Defensive Pistol Fundamentals

Gun Digest Book Of The Revolver

Shooter's Guide To Handguns

The 12 Essentials of Concealed Carry

Visit www.grantcunningham.com for more information

Praying Safe: The professional approach to protecting faith communities

By Grant Cunningham and Joshua Gideon

Published by Personal Security Institute LLC

Copyright 2018, Personal Security Institute LLC.

All rights reserved.

Click or visit:

www.prayingsafe.com